THE OLD-TIME ART OF Thrift ™

HOUSE of
WHITE
BIRCHES

PUBLISHERS
SINCE 1947

THE OLD-TIME ART OF Thrift™

Editors: Ken and Janice Tate
Copy Editor: Läna Schurb

Production Manager: Vicki Macy
Creative Coordinator: Shaun Venish
Design/Production Artist: Ken Tate
Traffic Coordinator: Sandra Beres
Production Assistants: Carol Dailey,
Cheryl Lynch, Chad Tate

Publishers: Carl H. Muselman, Arthur K. Muselman
Chief Executive Officer: John Robinson
Marketing Director: Scott Moss
Editorial Director: Vivian Rothe
Production Director: Scott Smith

Printed in the United States of America
First Printing: 1997
Library of Congress Number: 97-70768
ISBN: 1-882138-27-9

Dear Friends of the Good Old Days,

Thrift. That is one of those old-fashioned words you just don't hear very often anymore. The only time I hear it is when some secondhand shop is called a "Thrift Store."

The dictionary defines thrift as "an economical management of money or resources." I define it as an art that had its most beautiful work painted during the Good Old Days.

Think of it. Following the boom of "The Roaring Twenties," global depression set in. In the United States the Great Depression was ushered in with the stock market crash of 1929. What followed was a decade of deprivation the like of which this country has not seen before or since. Then, about the time the New Deal was taking hold, World War II brought more shortages—this time in support of the war effort.

Yet, the indomitable spirit of our people prevailed. During the '30s and '40s we figured out a way to make do.

When there was no material for making clothing, folks became creative. Wives and mothers used flour sacks and feed bags to make every conceivable piece of clothing from underwear outward. Hand-me-downs were refitted, resized, remade to make it through another child's school year. Cloth that couldn't be used any other way was made into aprons, washcloths, handkerchiefs—or finally recycled by way of the ragman for a few precious pennies.

Even when there was no money in the house for food, few went hungry. Most of us grew our own food in backyard gardens and ramshackle chicken coops. Summer kitchens churned out hundreds of jars of canned goods, from green beans to gooseberries. As long as the good Lord provided rain and shine we would never want for something on the table to eat.

Yes, whether it was making do or making our own fun, there was an art to how we made it back in those days. I hope these memories help you remember—or introduce you to—that Art of Thrift from the Good Old Days.

Sincerely,

Ken Tate

Editor

Contents

PINCHING PENNIES • 99

MAKING OUR OWN FUN • 129

Using It Up!

I'm a great putterer. Janice says so, and she knows me better than anyone. I putter around the tool shed. I putter around the barn. I putter around the garden. I putter around most anything that looks like it needs to be puttered around.

Puttering is an art that should be on the endangered species list—something seemingly doomed to extinction by a too-mobile society that has no room to move all of the accumulations of life. Modern houses don't have attics—they have crawl spaces. Puttering space is usually reduced to the garage, and the things you might putter with are routinely dispensed with the perennial "cleaning out of the garage."

Whenever I get a bit too melancholy, stir crazy or just too ornery to have around the house, Janice fixes it by suggesting, "Why don't you go out and putter around awhile?" She knows the psychological value of a good puttering session. It puts things in perspective. There is something about examining minutia that puts big things in order.

Once I asked Janice why she—and most women like her—don't putter. She retorted that women putter about the kitchen, putter with their knitting and crocheting, putter with their flowers. Men, she said, just refuse to recognize that as part of the art of puttering.

I, like most of you, grew up in hard times. There is something about not having much that makes you hold onto everything you do have. I have stored away dozens—if not hundreds—of relics of my childhood. Not that I'm sentimental, you understand. It's just I never know when I might need that old rotten piece of hemp with which Daddy taught me to rope—first fence posts and then calves.

I have every nail and board left over from the last renovation to the old family home. I have every extra screw, nut and bolt that has ever been included in packages of pantry shelves, pieces of office furniture or new tractor parts. Whenever I tuned up our now-antique pickup I always kept the old spark plugs and points, figuring I might need a spare set along the road someday. Much of this now inhabits a side shed in our barn—a musty old place near and dear to my heart.

I have said that my side shed is the equivalent to Janice's button box, where she rummages for the perfect button or snap for her latest project. She, of course, points out that her button box fits neatly in a drawer in her sewing cabinet, while my side shed looks like … well, you get the picture.

One old proverb from the tough Good Old Days gone by was: "Use it up, wear it out, make it do, or do without!" Part of using it up was holding onto it until some useful purpose made itself known.

Yes, I like to putter. And I'm blessed with having lived in the same place long enough to have plenty of places to putter. Just talking about it makes me want to go and see what I can find. Janice wanted a whatnot shelf for the bedroom, and I think I know right where I can get the board and wood screws for it.

It's a good thing I held onto all that junk. Otherwise today I'd be headed for the store instead of using it up.

—Ken Tate, Editor

The Mother of Recycling

By Bernice Lennart Classen

My folks took the family on a boat trip to Europe in 1947. My father hadn't been back to his native Sweden since 1910. When we approached the coastline of Scotland, we children teasingly told our mother that we saw the shores of her homeland. She was a Swede like my father, but she had the knack for knowing how to get her money's worth.

Even when the cupboard appeared to be rather bare, she still served a delicious, nutritious dinner—from out of nowhere, it seemed. We often looked in the refrigerator, and though it looked rather empty to us, she would whip up something very tasty.

When our clothing became worn, she zipped over to her sewing machine and quickly things would look almost new again. When mending a garment appeared to be hopeless, she put it in her big scrap bag. Later she used the accumulated scraps to make patchwork quilts and braided rugs. She also cut worn-out nylons into long strips and braided them into her rugs.

> *It was during the Great Depression, and nothing could be wasted. But Depression or not, Mother felt there was no excuse for wasting a crumb.*

It was during the Great Depression, and nothing could be wasted. But Depression or not, Mother felt there was no excuse for wasting a crumb.

I guess she took to heart John 6:12—the passage in the Good Book which recounts how Jesus fed the 5,000 with five loaves of bread and two small fishes, and then asked His disciples to gather up the leftover fragments so that nothing should be wasted.

At the height of the lean '30s she bleached empty sugar and flour sacks and sewed them into cute little school dresses. She dolled them up with colorful embroidery.

You know the price of your coffee today. Mother couldn't think of wasting an ounce of her beloved drink. She even had a use for those old coffee grounds. She seemed to have a sixth sense about which plants needed more humus (an ingredient in soil). She claimed that coffee grounds supplemented the humus. And she scattered leftover eggshells around the plants that needed calcium.

She picked fruit from her orchard. After sorting and washing it, she

peeled it, cored it and cut it up in pieces. Then she strung the pieces of fruit to dry in what she called her "hot room"—a little room behind her kitchen where the stove-pipe from her old-fashioned wood-burning range passed through to the chimney.

In addition to providing dried fruit for the children's snacks, Mother used it to make the yummiest, healthiest soup. She felt it was not only nutritious and economical, but surely saved on the use of laxatives.

Come butchering time, nothing was thrown away. Mother saw to it that those soup bones weren't wasted. Many were the winter days when she announced in her far-reaching voice, "Soup's on!" She rendered lard from hogs and used it in her baking. She made tasty sandwiches with homemade bread and head cheese.

But that isn't the end of this pig's "tale"— she also made soap from the rendered lard and lye. She claimed her soap could clean the dirtiest clothes. She made her own soap until the time of her death at age 80.

She had a compost pile where she collected peelings, cores and other food waste she couldn't use—anything the hogs wouldn't eat.

Mother didn't like to see milk wasted on our dairy farm, either. Other farmers might throw away the first few milkings from a newly freshened cow, or feed it to the dogs or calves, but she made a wonderfully rich custard from it.

Instead of spending scarce coins on floor wax during that memorable Depression, she used leftover skim milk. She had us put on Father's old woolen socks, and then we'd skid back and forth across the floor, polishing it. She killed two birds with one stone—the kids had fun, and she got the floors slicked up!

She churned her own butter then, and so we had yummy buttermilk to drink—I surely wish there were some "store-bought" like it!

She added the "starter" for the Swedish version of yogurt to milk, and it thickened. At lunch she served this with her hardtack, soup and perhaps some of her applesauce for dessert. We children enjoyed it, plus it was healthy as far as she was concerned. But though she might have been known as "the mother of recycling," she never gave anyone "leftover" love! ❖

Homemade Soap

By Charles B. O'Dooley

It was a warm, pleasant night in early June and we were sitting on the porch, shelling early peas for the next day's dinner.

The year was 1933. As we sat enjoying the evening, Mom said, "Kids, tomorrow we will make soap." The next morning we built a fire under the copper kettle in the back yard. Mom had us bring out stone jars of homemade lard.

Soap-making was a way of life in those days, as well as an economical factor. Today's women can still save money by making soap, using bacon grease they've saved along with other grease they use to fry food. Step by step, here is how to make your own soap.

The ingredients you will need are: 1 can lye, 5 cups water and 6 pounds grease

If you weigh the grease in a can or jar, be sure to deduct the weight of the container so you have 6 pounds of grease. Also, before you weigh it, you should strain your bacon grease and any other fat to get rid of any impurities.

You'll need a large pot to make soap in this quantity. If you prefer, cut the amounts of ingredients in half. Add the lye to the water and bring it to the boil. Then lower the heat until the mixture is just simmering.

Stir the mixture constantly until the lye is completely dissolved. Then add the grease, continuing to stir until the mixture is thick, like jelly. This will take 20–25 minutes.

After the mixture has thickened, pour it into a shallow cake pan and place it in a cool place to harden overnight. Then cut it into squares. It will not get as hard as store-bought soap, but will stay somewhat soft.

While it is cooking, the soap will give off a strong but clean odor. If you prefer, add some kind of perfume to the soap while it's cooking. Use any scent that appeals to you. ❖

Haircuts & Resoled Shoes

By Barbara Carrothers

Remember home-style haircuts and shoes resoled, sometimes by the repairman and sometimes by a member of the immediate family? If you are over 60 years old, you probably do.

I remember one haircut which somehow the entire family managed to get into. The family had gathered at Gram's for Sunday dinner and Aunt Viola decided I needed a haircut. She determined to do it herself and save Gram the price of a haircut. She put Gram's big apron around my neck and started snipping with a none-too-sharp pair of shears.

I wore my hair in a Dutch-boy cut, and it should have been a simple matter to follow it around my head. It didn't turn out that way. She couldn't get the sides even.

At that point, Aunt Esther got in the act and tried to even it up. When she didn't succeed, my oldest cousin, Mildred, tried her luck—which wasn't much better than the aunts'. My other cousin, Camille, being too young to be trusted with the shears, perched on a stool and offered advice and remarks about how I looked.

When they finally turned me loose, I looked like one of those chickens that have topknots on their heads. My hair was way above my ears! And my ears stuck out like the handles on a sugar bowl. To add insult to injury, they all trotted out into the yard for a group snapshot. They might have let me wear a hat, like a stocking cap pulled way down!

"The tops are still good." I can still hear Gram say that, and it meant I was to take the shoes to the store repairman.

Mr. Davis was a good repairman, but a resoled shoe just isn't what it once was! The new soles were thick and stiff, and they squeaked!

There was no sneaking into the schoolroom or Sunday school with a pair of newly resoled shoes squeaking like an unused door. Every head turned my way, and the teacher frowned mightily.

I learned early to head for a shallow mud puddle or wet grass to stop the squeak. One time a relative who had a repair outfit set up in his basement offered to do the job for free.

When I saw the finished job, I gulped. Somewhere he had gotten a pulley belt that looked like it was an inch thick. I felt like I was on stilts, and I smelled like oil for ages. ❖

Making the Most of Wood

By Martin Hullender

Wood—where would we be without it? During the average person's lifetime, he or she uses the products from 400 trees. There is little doubt that wood is probably more closely interwoven with the life of man than any other single material. From cradle to coffin, wood is a constant companion.

I wouldn't be at all surprised if my brother and I climbed more than 400 trees down on the farm. Our favorite climbing tree was a yellow poplar not far from our house. We dearly loved to climb that old poplar. We'd climb to the top and ride with the wind. What fun for a growing boy! Possibly some of our happiest hours were spent climbing trees. We did a lot of fancy dreaming in the top of that friendly tree while the balmy breeze blew through our hair.

We boys looked forward with great pleasure to Sunday afternoon, especially in the spring and autumn. Instead of taking a nap after dinner at noon, Dad would take us to the woods. Sometimes we didn't go far; then again, we might go several miles. Sometimes we walked across several farms. Occasionally we would go down in the pasture, near the springs. A branch—brook—ran along the edge of the field. There were lots of shade trees—willows, elders, alders, a few small oaks and pines.

> *Our favorite climbing tree was a yellow poplar not far from our house. We dearly loved to climb that old poplar.*

In those days every man and boy carried a pocketknife of some kind. When I was given my first knife, Dad taught me how to sharpen it and care for it. To keep it clean, I always kept my knife in a pocket separate from the many, many other things that a growing boy carries in his pockets.

What Dad could do with a knife was almost endless! First he showed us how to play mumbly peg. Of course, he used an old knife for this. Then Dad would make a little water wheel, support and all, from branches and bits of wood from a fallen tree. He rigged it up across the brook where the water ran over the rocks in a little waterfall. If we went through a cornfield on the way to the pasture, Dad would cut a cornstalk and make a cornstalk fiddle.

In the springtime while the sap was rising, Dad would cut a maple twig about the size of his forefinger and make a whistle. He'd make a canoe to float down the brook from willow or hickory twigs.

On a hot summer day we would put a handful of oak, maple or poplar leaves in our hats—good protection against sunstroke.

The sweet-smelling leaves were nice as the sweat dropped down into our faces.

Mother gave us the empty spools from her sewing machine.

When Dad whittled small pegs, inserted one in each end of the spool and then cut the spools in half through the middle, two small tops resulted.

I don't remember ever seeing Dad just whittling for the heck of it, though whittling was an art in itself. He thought that while he was whittling, he might as well make something useful or ornamental.

Dad always liked to work with wood, whether with the knife, ax, saw or drawknife. We were taught these things too, although we never became as adept as Dad.

He could take his ax, go into the woods, and bring out enough logs to make a smokehouse or corncrib. He hewed the logs on the sides to square them, notched them, and with only a little help, up the building would go.

To cut shingles, we went back into the woods and selected a tree about 26 inches in diameter. We felled it with a crosscut saw—if you don't believe that's a job, try it sometime! Then we cut off sawing blocks 2 feet long.

Here's where Dad ran into trouble. Robert and I made out fairly well because we were nearly the same weight, but because there was quite a difference between Dad's weight and mine, I'm afraid he caught the heavy end of the job. He said he didn't so much mind me riding the saw.

"But, son," he said, "if you're going to ride the saw, please take your feet off the ground. Quit dragging them."

We split the 2-foot-long blocks into quarters. Then the work of making boards would start. Dad used a small maul and a froe (frow) to drive the boards. This was tiring work, but after a while he had enough boards for the job at hand.

Many times I've seen Dad run his hand over a piece of cedar or hickory or ash on which he was working. He felt it as a woman would feel a piece of cloth when she goes to the store to buy a dress, or as a horse trader runs his hand over a horse as he evaluates it.

At one time Dad made us a baseball bat out of a piece of hickory. Boy oh boy, was that bat a honey! It was a bit heavy for a small boy, but a larger boy could wham that ball way yonder!

Many small objects around the house and barn were the products of Dad's work with a knife or ax.

When he wanted a trough for the animals, down would come a small tree which Dad hewed out to suit his purpose.

Dad taught us that we should never cut down a tree unless it was to serve a useful purpose. He seemed to be on good terms with trees. He knew the names of all the trees, shrubs, vines, weeds and grasses, and throughout his life he made the most out of each tree he used. ❖

Whittling

By John B. Montgomery

Whittling is a unique way to create and relax with minimal money and space. Go find your favorite pocketknife, cut a green branch from a smooth-bark tree, sit on a comfortable chair, turn on relaxing music, and you are ready to experience the pleasure of creating and the satisfaction of saying, "I made that."

This project is the prevailing standby—the whistle. Whittling a whistle takes less time than watching a movie, and is less expensive, especially if you already own a pocketknife. The materials and tools lists, as well as the instructions and diagrams, are brief and basic. Feel free to improvise or try your own rustic artistry on the whistle.

Tools
1. Pocketknife—a sharp 2- or 3-inch blade
2. An oil stone or whetstone
3. Comfortable chair or bench

Materials
Limb or branch approximately ½ inch in diameter from a smooth-bark tree—willow, poplar, basswood and sycamore are best, but several others may be substituted.

Instructions
1. Cut through the bark to the solid wood 1 or 2 inches from the end.
2. Wet the branch and then pound the longer end all over.
3. Take hold of both ends and twist and pull the stick out from the bark. Repeat pounding if it doesn't come out.
4. Put the stick back in the bark to prevent breakage and cut the notch and tapering mouthpiece.
5. Remove stick again from the bark and cut the end off flush with the base of the notch.
6. Slice some of the wood off of the plug from the air passage.
7. Replace the plug in the mouthpiece.
8. Cut off another piece of wood to plug the other end. Caution: Use a temporary plug to determine the length of the air chamber. Too long or short and you can't hear the frequencies.
9. Blow the whistle.
10. A pea or similar object in the barrel will produce a warble in the whistle.

If you are more adventurous, you may make a sliding plug to vary the pitch and timbre like a trombone. Or, drill two or more holes in the barrel and vary the sound like a flute.

Hints
Leave approximately 2 or 3 inches of air chamber for the air to resonate. A normal person can only hear frequencies from 16 to 20,000 cycles per second, so keep adjusting the end plug until you can hear the whistle.

If you cannot obtain a green limb, use a dowel rod. Drill a hole lengthwise for a smaller dowel rod and carve whatever design you wish on the exterior. The instructions and diagrams are the same as the other.

Whistle Diagram

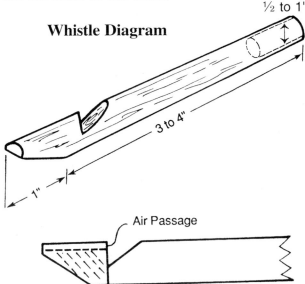

½ to 1"

3 to 4"

1"

Air Passage

Mama's Wonderful Christmas Trees

By Lois Smith

Kids nowadays must think of Christmas trees as factory-made tinsel-decked objects which come in a box and are folded up and put away after the day has passed.

We have one in our house each holiday season and, attractive and glowing as it is, it will never be able to crowd out of my memory the first Christmas trees of my childhood.

We were tenant farmers, poor as church mice. Mom and Dad were married during the depths of the Depression; they sold their first tobacco crop for a whopping 3 cents a pound. My first Christmas must have been pretty bleak, at least by today's standards.

I don't remember much about the gifts I did or didn't receive, but I do remember Mama's wonderful Christmas trees. There were no satin balls or velvet ribbon bows or lights which blinked on and off. There were no imported glass ornaments, and there was not even 1 inch of tinsel. What there was was the product of Mama's ingenuity and her desire to teach me the spirit of Christmas.

Decorating the tree was something Mama kept in mind all year long. Whenever she came across some trinket that had possibilities, she tucked it away to wait for the Yule season. She had been collecting things years before her marriage, but when I was barely 2, the house burned down, taking her precious box of Christmas ornaments with it. Mama had to come up with some new decorations, and what she came up with, as I remember, resulted in the most beautiful Christmas trees I ever saw.

The first year after the fire, Mama went to the grocery store a few days before Christmas and bought 3 or 4 pounds of orange, red, green and yellow gumdrops. When she got them home, she wrapped each sugary piece in its own little cellophane square and tied it with a length of bright yarn, leaving a loop. Her tree decoration was ready.

I still remember how the cellophane sparkled with orange and red and yellow and green light from the gumdrops. To my child's eyes it was magnificent.

When Christmas was over, Mama carefully tucked away her "new" decorations in a box to await the next holiday season.

The next year she added English walnut shells to our decorations. Before painting the shells she carefully cracked the nuts into perfect halves, removed the nut meats and then glued the halves together, inserting a hanging string between them first. She painted the shells in many bright colors. And so nutshells joined the gumdrops on Mama's trees.

When I grew big enough to help, Mama had me cut bright pictures from magazines, snip them into strips, and fashion a long, long paper chain which she looped 'round and 'round the tree in graceful, sweeping scallops. Plus, we now had electricity. Our trees could be lighted, and they took on a decidedly "uptown" look.

Mama was pleased that we no longer had to make do with improvised decorations, and that at last we could afford some of the "finer things" other people put on their trees. But what Mama didn't completely understand was that all the fancy baubles ever hung on the world's most spectacular trees could never hold the joy and wonder I found in hand-painted walnut shells and cellophane-wrapped gumdrops. ❖

We Saved String

By Marion Odmark

*W*ould you believe that string was once a household necessity—and that it was saved as carefully as money? There was hardly a family emergency in my day that didn't call for a piece of string—to pull stubborn baby teeth with the kitchen doorknob, for kites and bicycle handlebars, tops and ponytails, to wrap too-large rings, and of course to wrap and carry packages.

There was hardly a family that didn't save string. In fact, I never heard of anyone actually buying string until I was in high school (class of '30). A friend said she wanted to stop at the hardware store to buy—of all things—string!

Good grief! I thought. *What kind of a home life does the poor girl have? No string!*

My whole life has been tied up with string. String was my first taste of responsibility, my first real job. When I was 5 years old, Nanny and Mother put me in charge of our string drawer, in the pantry off the kitchen in Nanny's big old house where we

lived. Nanny had come there as a bride during the Civil War. The string drawer was always stuck—warped, perhaps, or maybe it just never did fit properly. At any rate, the string drawer couldn't be pulled all the way out, or pushed all the way back.

In this drawer we kept all the loose string. Because I had the only hand small enough to get in it, I was put in sole charge of this department. Plus, I had the special talent the job demanded; Mother and Nanny said they had never seen anybody with such a talent for untying knots. Flattery went a long way then (as now). If there was any tangled or knotted string, I got it first and, with the officious pride of the very young, valiantly did my duty.

Every so often the string drawer was cleaned out and the pieces wound tightly into balls which were carefully stored away in the string cupboard off the playroom. Around our house, this string cupboard compared favorably to the fruit cellar in terms of family security. It was nice to know you had plenty of string handy for whatever need might arise.

A few years later when I was 9 or 10, a great windfall came our way. Uncle George bought a cotton mill and sent over dozens and dozens of spindles of new string! Nanny, Mother, my sister Betty and I stared at this mountain of string as if it were a Christmas tree.

"Just look at all that beautiful string!" we marveled. "Think of all the things we can do with it!"

This unexpected bounty did not make the string drawer and string cupboard obsolete, however. Used string would still be saved. But with the thousands of yards of unbroken, unknotted string, we went into a new flurry of production.

We crocheted and tatted and knitted bedspreads, antimacassars, nut cups, luncheon sets, pot holders, socks, hats, sweaters, bed jackets, dresses, handbags and trimmings for sheets, pillowcases and hankies. We emptied the neighborhood grocery of its Rit and Tintex dyes to color our string creations. We experimented with mixing our own colors, resulting in some strange hues never seen before or since. We saved leftover coffee to tint doilies ecru. All that string was converted into practical items.

As time passed, I still had a possessive and personal feeling about string. I sighed with Henry Sambrooke Leigh's verse, "My love, she is a kitten, and my heart's a ball of string"; I giggled at girls who "had a fellow on a string" and at boys who would "string the girls along."

I hummed to *I've Got the World on a String* and shared Hilaire Belloc's image: "The chief defect of Henry King was chewing little bits of string." And when *Reader's Digest* ran an item about an eccentric lady who kept a box labeled "String too short to save," I felt I had met a kindred spirit.

When I reached those impressionable teen-age years, there was talk about a young bachelor who was much sought by Chicago society as a very amusing guest. To get the conversational ball rolling at a dinner party he'd inquire of his partner, "Do you like string?" He said he could wrap up an entire personality picture by the reply.

He was heartened if someone replied, "It depends on what kind of string." He was saddened by those who said, "Not very much," and he dismissed as conventional bores those who responded, "Forgive me, did you say string?" He certainly sounded like a lot of fun to me. I dreamed of meeting him—and finding love at first sight.

Years later when I was studying psychology, I chuckled at an analogy William James used in *Principles of Psychology*—that learning new habits is like someone winding a ball of string: "If he should accidentally drop the ball and watch it unwind on the floor, there would be no sense in sitting down to bewail the fact. He should recognize that while the twine had unrolled a little, he had made a good start. He would pick up the ball and go to work again, winding the string with undiminished patience and hope."

When transparent gummed tape came on the market, I grandly predicted that it would never catch on. Granted, the tape made neat packages, and was very serviceable, and saved time for the salespeople and those elves hidden behind sales counters.

But it was all too obvious that you couldn't hook your finger in tape to carry a parcel as you could with string. More important, you couldn't save tape to use again.

Thrifty homemakers unaccustomed to buying string certainly wouldn't spend good money for this new gimmick!

That was the last prediction I ever made. ❖

The Old Fireplace

By Celia Brown

All the work is done. The builders have just finished our new fireplace. It is a thing of beauty—and a far cry from the one I knew in my childhood. We are proud of our new fireplace, and certainly the old river rock fireplace of my youth would look out of place in our new home. But I'm sure there will be times when I will look back with longing to the fireside evenings of long ago.

The leaping blazes, the enveloping warmth, and finally the glowing embers brought comfort to our tired bodies. But the shared pleasures of a winter evening, as our large family spent hours together in congenial and pleasant pastimes, brought peace and comfort to the soul.

While Father strummed the old guitar, we sang together in the firelight—old-time ballads, spirituals, and the popular ragtime favorites. Checkers, chess, dominoes and Monopoly filled many an evening.

There were also other games, unknown by today's children. Who

The leaping blazes, the enveloping warmth, and finally the glowing embers brought comfort to our tired bodies.

remembers Lotto, Telca, and the favorite with the homemade board game, Nine-Man-Morris? We drew the game chart on a big piece of cardboard and used buttons, beans or grains of corn for the playing pieces which we moved from station to station.

There were also many card games: whist, Authors, even Old Maid. Authors introduced me to literature, and the names of many of those well-known writers and what they wrote have stayed with me to today.

There was usually a quiet hour of reading aloud before bedtime, and this was a very cherished portion of our evening. As far back as I can remember, Father did the reading while Mother sat with her darning or knitting. As we children advanced with our reading ability, we also took turns at the reading. James Fenimore Cooper, Charles Dickens, Robert Louis Stevenson, and even Victor Hugo and Tolstoy were favorites.

There was usually an old flatiron on the hearth where a little one or two was busy cracking hickory nuts, hazelnuts or black walnuts. When the fire had burned down, one of the girls would bring out the long-handled, wire-screen corn popper. Soon the fragrance of fresh popcorn tempted us all. A bowl of polished apples was always at hand on the center table.

We were fortunate to have an Aladdin kerosene lamp. It cast clear white light over the group, allowing needlework and reading without undue eye strain.

Without modern woodcutting tools, cutting and hauling our winter wood supply was a tremendous task. Those wide fireplaces used an enormous amount of wood, and the huge kitchen stove required its share, too. But I don't remember ever hearing Father or my brothers complain about that chore. Wood was plentiful then; its only cost was the labor of cutting and hauling it. Piling up 15 cords of wood was simply accepted as a necessary effort, albeit a heavy one.

Our fireplace was built by the middle-aged couple who had homesteaded the place in 1903. Building it was an off-season job for the stonemason. His wife stayed with the place and held down the homestead while he went away to work to earn the money for building and making improvements.

During a slack season in his work, he accumulated the rock for the fireplace, taking it from the riverbed that ran through the place. With infinite care and patience, he fitted the flat rocks together to make an attractive, long-lasting source of heat for the big living room. After more than 90 years, it still serves well.

Today there are gadgets on the market that roll old newspapers tightly so they can be used as fireplace logs. Packages of mixed chemicals can also be purchased which, when sprinkled onto the paper logs in the fireplace, produce brilliant colors in the flames.

We enjoyed the same treat, but ours was the old-fashioned, do-it-yourself method, which provided much pleasure during the holidays. Papers and magazines were not very plentiful, but when we had some, we rolled them as tightly as we could, making rolls about 5 inches in diameter. Then we placed the rolls in the same 10-gallon stone crock we'd used for making sauerkraut in the fall.

Over the logs we poured our homemade chemical solution—a mixture of 5 cups rock salt and 5 cups coloring chemical for every 3 gallons of water. The logs had to be submerged while they soaked in it. After soaking two weeks, they were laid out to dry. If laid in the sun, it doesn't take very long, but without sunshine, it takes about six weeks.

Recently, while leafing through my mother's old "receipt" book, I came across her formulas for making the chemical solution for soaking paper logs. There, in her spidery script, I found the particulars about the chemicals, as well as some warnings.

Rock salt, I read, produced yellow flames. The reds are made by lithium compounds. Strontium compounds produce scarlet flames. Calcium compounds make orange.

Any copper compounds except chloride produce green. A combination of thallium and tellurium makes a very pure green, while barium compounds make a yellowish green. Potassium compounds yield violet or purple, as do rubidium and cesium compounds.

We hoarded every scrap to make logs for the holiday season. We enjoyed the colorful flames much more then because such a fire was special, and not to be enjoyed all winter long.

This winter we will burn paper logs rolled on a clever little metal gadget some smart person invented. We will sprinkle them with chemicals that come in a little envelope.

Then two lonely old people will sit before the open flames and toast their shins while they wonder what the children and grandchildren are doing. And perhaps they will reminisce a little about the good old days when families gathered on winter evenings and enjoyed a bit of music, some good reading, the healthy competition of games, home-grown snacks instead of junk food, and the real solidarity of family life. ❖

Grandma Was A Rare Ecologist

By Mabel Dickson Short

Grandma was a rare ecologist, but—bless her heart—she never knew it. In fact, I doubt that Grandma ever heard the word in her whole lifetime of 75 years. But when I recall all the make-do things she knew about, I know she was well ahead of her time—and a rare ecologist.

For instance, take the thousand-and-one times she plucked the feathers from her old Rhode Island Red hens and the Dominique rooster—she called him something that sounded like "Dominecker"—and made soft, downy beds for her family. Grandma never heard the words "innerspring mattress."

Grandma would have reveled in a visit to one of our city dumps. I'll wager the average modern family carts off more good things to the city dump than Grandma ever owned in her whole lifetime.

She knew that if she didn't take care of what she had, she wouldn't have even that very long.

Grandma was a farmer's wife and she specialized in the thrifty use of resources. She would have sputtered disgustedly over the word "ecology." But she knew that if she didn't take care of what she had, she wouldn't have even that very long.

Talk about inventors! Grandma was the greatest! She didn't have a laboratory to conduct tests, or a mahogany desk behind which she could study and do her research. Her only research was searching for a way to use every common item at hand.

The old sadirons did double duty, pressing Grandpa's Sunday britches and her own go-to-meetin' dress (she didn't have time to iron everyday clothes), plus acting as a doorstop on her air conditioner. Yes, Grandma had air conditioners, the greatest model since the beginning of time—the front and back doors, which she kept propped open in summer, to create a draft through the house.

And Grandma was a great one for keeping everything oiled and running. There was no place for rusty clocks, crosscut saws or sloweddown kids around the farm. There was too much to be done—and too much castor oil in the general store right down the road, she said pointedly. She vowed that that kind of lubrication would make anything start off in high gear, notwithstanding the fact that the outhouse (she called it "the closet") was 100 yards from the main house. Why the distance? She wanted no flies buzzing around the house.

And speaking of flies. … As there were no screens, come a damp summer day, a swarm of flies always came from somewhere. (She was certain they were not from the closet.) What did Grandma do? She marched out to the peach tree by the well house (while every one of her young 'uns held their breath), and brought in a nice bushy limb.

Then, while Grandpa and nine kids ate dinner, she stood and swished the flies away with the leafy branch, waving it slowly and endlessly above corn pone, black-eyed peas, ham and sweet potatoes.

But don't be misled—Grandma didn't waste that limb, even when it became too dry for a fly chaser. When the leaves began to fall off she carefully stripped it down and placed it high over the back door where the kids couldn't reach it. Later—and pity the kid who committed a misdemeanor—she applied it to the seat of the britches, where it still did a world of good. Grandma simply didn't waste anything.

And come wash day? Grandma called it "Blue Monday." Her washing machine went into action down by the well house. Oh, yes, she had a washing machine even in those days. Its brand name was The Old Battlin' Block. It was an old tree stump on which she placed lye-soaped clothes. Then, using a wide paddle with a short handle, she whammed the daylights out of those clothes until they were sparkling clean and germ free. What germ could survive such a pounding? What always amazes me, however, is how the family ever had anything but rags to wear after all that whaling.

As soon as the wash was all hung out on the barbed-wire fence—plus a few overalls on the tree limbs—Grandma turned her boundless energy to the floors. Grandma had beautifully polished floors, and without wax. She had never heard of rugs or linoleum, but weekly polishing with that strong lye-soap water from her washtubs left her pine floors white and clean.

Of course, her vicious scrubbing might finish off the old sagebrush broom, but she knew where more were stored in the barn. Each year when the sagebrush dried, she had her boys go down and cut a load, tie it in bundles and stack them in the barn loft.

Yes, in those days boys had other things to do besides running around the country getting into mischief. Grandma believed in putting all that pent-up boyish vitality to good use in a way that met her needs and kept the boys out of trouble. One of her favorite quotations was, "An idle mind is the devil's workshop." Grandma made sure that this didn't happen often, but when it did, the panacea for such transgressions waited ready in the woodshed.

Grandma saved all newspapers. Grandpa believed in keeping up with the world news, so there were always lots of papers around. But Grandma needed lots. She cut many into squares for the outhouse, especially when the old catalogs were used up.

Then every summer, after the garden stuff was all canned or dried, she went into action. She knew how to make paste as well as pancakes from flour. Using all that newspaper that was stacked in the smokehouse, she rejuvenated the whole house with another coat of newspapers on the walls. I wish I knew how many coats of newspaper covered the walls of that old farmhouse; Grandma always said another coat would keep out a little more wind.

One could sit in the bedroom and read about the new styles for last year, or sit in the kitchen and read about a lynching that took place in Georgia. Across the hall in another room, you could learn how the war was progressing. Grandma said that since she couldn't do anything about these problems anyway, she didn't mind reading about them a year late.

Grandma learned many things from experience. She learned, for instance, that a plate of biscuits or baked sweet potatoes set in the safe for supper could disappear instantly once nine kids made a midafternoon raid.

She also learned that a wonderful pacifier for the baby could be made by buttering a piece of bread, sprinkling it with sugar, tying it in a bit of cloth and placing it in the baby's mouth. (Had I ever tried it, my baby would have swallowed the thing and choked to death. Maybe I just wasn't an ecologist like Grandma.)

Grandma also learned a lot of shortcuts, such as pulling a kid's tooth by tying one end of a string to the tooth and the other end to a doorknob, and then slamming the door. She also knew how to make toothbrushes from hackberry twigs by chewing them until they were soft. She knew how to make dolls for her little girls out of corncobs, dressing them from her scrap bag.

And speaking of scraps, she wasted nary a one. She sewed them together, often in 1-inch squares, and made quilts from them.

Grandma could find more uses for a hairpin than Carter had liver pills. She used them to thread through kids' frazzled shoelaces, clean out ears, scratch where it itched, clean under fingernails, and even tie little things together.

I don't suppose Grandma ever heard of a clothes hanger. But one whole wall in what she called her "side room" was lined with wooden

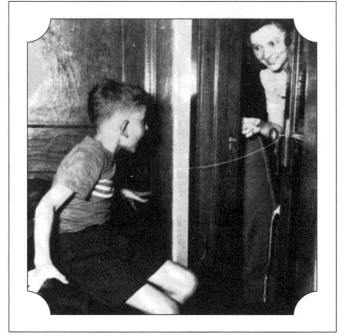

pegs on which were hung the few changes of clothes the family owned.

Grandma saved matches by "banking" coals in the fireplace in winter. She carried a blaze to the old wood-burning cookstove by using a rolled-up newspaper for a torch. (I guess she always saved back a few newspapers from wallpapering and the outhouse for this use.)

In winter she showed her little girls how to make doll beds from shoe boxes, and in summer she showed them how to make a playhouse in the woods, using broken dishes and glass for play dishes and piles of leaves for beds.

She showed her little boy how to make a home for the little turtle he found from a shoe box, and she showed him how and where to prepare a worm bed so they could fish in the nearby creek where sun perch abounded.

Grandma simply didn't waste a thing. When a sheet wore thin in the middle, she split it in half, sewed the selvedge edges together, hemmed the sides, and presto! She had another sheet for the children's beds and the cradle—and she needed plenty.

She made towels from heavy feed sacks to catch the weekday grime from the field. On Sundays, a white towel hung on the back porch by the wash pan and water bucket, but come Monday morning it hit the old battlin' block and was again replaced by a sack towel.

And do you think Grandma would waste money for a store-bought dipper? Not on your tintype—not as long as she could raise gourds in the garden.

Yes, my Grandma was an ecologist of the rarest sort. And I guess it is just as well she never knew it, for she would have scoffed at the idea. Ecologist indeed! ❖

Fuel Shortage!

By Eula Newsome

Perhaps the first fuel shortage occurred soon after men learned the benefits of fire. There have always been places where there was nothing with which to build or sustain a fire. Barren deserts offer neither peat nor coal nor wood, but in most parts of the world, there is some natural resource that can be used to generate warmth.

People today live in fear of a fuel shortage. Seventy years ago, on a bleak prairie homestead, we endured a wild blizzard with tightly twisted prairie hay as our only source of heat. How welcome was the soft Chinook wind that followed, taking the snow and baring the ground so we could gather buffalo chips. They burned quickly and created great amounts of ashes, but they furnished enough heat for cooking and even for heating the oven for the great loaves of bread which were the backbone of our family's diet.

A year later the family was in better circumstances. "Fuel shortage"

Cow chips and buffalo chips were a common substitute for fuel on the treeless prairie. This photograph was taken on a lonely part of the Great Plains in Nebraska.

was not a familiar term in those days. Father was working on the railroad section, and had obtained a large pile of discarded railroad ties—good, hard wood that would burn well and not too fast.

With forethought, Father had piled the ties so they could be rolled one at a time onto a pair of sawhorses beside them. Father would be working away from home throughout the winter, which meant that Mother would be the one who would have to saw the ties to stove length and bring them into the home-stead cabin to provide fuel during the long, cold months.

Her saw was an old carpenter's saw and the work was tedious, but there was no alternative. Her small children must be kept warm. Those ties were the only fuel, and Mother was the only one who could saw it and carry the chunks into the cabin. Piled neatly beside the door, they were insurance against a sudden blizzard. It was a hardship, but Mother did not recognize a "fuel shortage."

As the homestead developed, there was evidence of slightly increasing prosperity. Coal, used as sparingly as possible, was hauled out from Sidney, and cow chips, buffalo chips, twisted hay and railroad ties were used only as stopgaps when the coal supply ran low.

The day came when the final papers were received. The homestead had "proved up," and the land was theirs. Now Father felt free to indulge his love of change. To him, the flat prairie had never been home. We would go to Arkansas—cheap land, and plenty of trees and hills.

For three years we reveled in the abundance of easily procured fuel: huge oak logs for the vast fireplace, gnarled chunks for the heating stove, lengths of just the proper size for cooking, and beautiful hickory chips for smok-ing our pork. During those years I never saw my mother return from a walk in the woods without her gingham apron gathered up and filled with bits and chips of wood.

I think she regretted the fact that the woods were full of lovely fuel that would eventually rot down into the soil because she couldn't use it all. There was no fuel shortage. But this, too, came to an end.

Itchy feet took us to the plains of eastern Colorado. Coal was high in price. Twenty-three miles was a long haul for a man who was busy planting corn and raising hogs.

There were no trees and no railroad ties—but there were corn-cobs. And as long as there were plenty of corncobs, there was no fuel shortage.

There were four teen-age girls in our home, and two large galvanized washtubs. We brought in corncobs in relays, going out in pairs with a washtub between us, filling the tub with frozen cobs and bringing them back into the house. When one pair returned, the other pair left with the second tub. By nightfall, both tubs were full, ready for the morning fire.

Gathering frozen, mud-covered corncobs from a hog pen is an experience denied to most people. "Not a bad job at all," Father assured us, sitting beside the stove with the current issue of the county paper. "It isn't as though there are only two of you. Two can sit by the fire and get warm while the other two gather a load of fuel." There wasn't really a fuel shortage.

The hogs ate diligently, and the cobs were collected, but eventually it became clear that the crop of cobs would not outlast the winter. So one crisp, clear morning, the eldest son was sent into town with the team and wagon to "bring out a jag" of coal to supplement the cobs.

The wind rose in late afternoon, driving an occasional snowflake. Father looked at the sky with a discerning eye. "It looks like a blizzard, but John should be getting in any minute with the coal." Though it was becoming difficult to find enough cobs, by the time dark came we had two full tubs—but John had not returned with the coal, and the storm had intensified.

Now a new problem presented itself. Mother had 200 baby chicks in the brooder house. A coal-burning brooder stove kept the little room comfortably warm. A big scuttle of fine coal had been kept exclusively for the brooder fire, but the weather had been colder than expected and now the coal was gone. We girls decided we would stay up all night, taking turns, and keep the fire going with corncobs. We couldn't bear to see Mother's chicks chill to death.

But our hopes were soon dashed. The wet, frozen cobs smoldered and sizzled in the stove, but they didn't burn. But Mother's lovely little chicks had to be saved. We appealed to Father.

"There's only one thing to do. Carry a couple of baskets of corn to the brooder house, and burn that." Then, responding to our looks of consternation, he continued, "I remember the winter of 1878 in Kansas. Corn was 17 cents a bushel and coal was so high no settler could afford it. Corn was cheaper than coal, and it was right at hand, so we burned corn."

Again there was no fuel shortage, but we girls flinched every time we dropped a few of the beautiful golden ears into the brooder stove. The corn made such a terrific fire that it was difficult to keep the heat as low as it should have been. With the damper closed, we took turns sitting in a kitchen chair beside the stove, watching our little charges.

The storm did not develop into a blizzard, and sometime during the night John pulled in with a skimpy load of coal. When we visited the hog pen, the swine were busily chomping corn. The cobs were beginning to accumulate, and we

There was not yet a real fuel shortage. There was lots of corn—which meant lots of cobs—and spring was not far away.

picked them up to supplement the coal. There was not yet a real fuel shortage. There was lots of corn—which meant lots of cobs—and spring was not far away.

Our next trek was to the panhandle of Idaho where cut-over timberland promised plenty of wood to burn. We were not disappointed. Our "stump ranch" sat right in the heart of a long stretch of second-growth timber—white pine, yellow pine, cedar, larch, hemlock, maple and alder. Timber harvesting was becoming more mechanized.

A "Swede saw" could be used to cut stove wood, and a two-man crosscut was the standard tool for felling trees, but gasoline-powered chain saws were coming into extensive use, cutting down on time and labor.

We still needed axes, wedges and splitting mauls to prepare our stove wood, but if one did not fear work, there was no fuel shortage.

There were those seeking the easy way out who used kerosene stoves for cooking. It was less work, and cooler during the summer. Some used natural or bottled gas. That was the time the REA came into being; even isolated rural folk looked forward to having electric lights and other conveniences. Small thought was given to the need to develop the vast amount of electricity the country would eventually need. It was hard to imagine a fuel shortage.

Many years have passed. We have plenty of wood, but oldsters find the sawing, chopping and splitting too strenuous. A small electric stove takes care of all the cooking I cannot do in the trusty fireless cooker.

And this winter, we came back—full circle—to free fuel for the home. The local senior citizens collect newspapers from the townsfolk, then roll them into 30-pound rolls and sell them to local florists for flower wrappings. They are happy to have people like us to haul away the papers they can't use.

We tie these discards into tight rolls and find that they make fine fireplace "logs"; they burn slowly and give off a surprising amount of heat. We have no fuel shortage! ❖

We Beat One Energy Crunch

By Mary Wells Geer

Four or five people in our town will admit they have lived long enough to remember Pearl Harbor and will testify to the "energy crunch" we experienced between 1942 and 1945. Finding gasoline for sale at the pump was almost impossible in spite of strict government rationing. Buying enough fuel for a rare trip beyond the city limits meant weeks of hoarding those precious ration stamps which had to be forfeited for each legitimate gallon pumped into the tank.

We finally retired our full-size automobile in the name of patriotism, putting it up on blocks "for the duration." We replaced it with a small, home-built three-wheeler that resembled a golf cart. It was a bit conspicuous, but it got us—two adults and two small boys—to work, church, the grocery, Cub Scout meetings and, thanks to one enterprising neighbor, into the pages of *Popular Mechanics*. The vehicle consumed very little gasoline, and we managed nicely on our few ration coupons.

Then we heard about a clever handyman from Arizona (the friend of a friend of a friend) who had begun to manufacture an inexpensive gadget which could convert a full-size, gasoline-powered automobile into a diesel-burning vehicle. We bought one of the gadgets sight unseen. Taking our car down off the blocks and faithfully following the mimeographed instructions, we made the conversion, adding a diesel carburetor alongside the gas carburetor, and installing a second tank in the trunk where we could hold low-grade diesel fuel or kerosene.

Eager to try our new diesel chariot, we located a filling station and bravely called, "Fill 'er up!" after pointing out the extra tank in the trunk.

According to the brochure, the trick was to lead the low-grade fuel through a metal tube inside the hot exhaust manifold in order to vaporize the diesel oil just before it entered the engine through the carburetor. The gadget they'd sold us for about $40 turned out to be a replacement for the factory-installed manifold which contained the necessary tubing. We scrounged the auxiliary copper tubing and the extra fuel tank from a Los Angeles junkyard.

Eager to try our new diesel chariot, we located a filling station and bravely called, "Fill 'er up!" after pointing out the extra tank in the trunk. We were joyous about making this fuel purchase without surrendering a single coupon!

But we soon learned that the brochure had failed to include driving instructions for our "new" two-accelerator, two-carburetor, choice-of-fuels vehicle. Fortunately there was no great network of freeways in 1942, so we could learn slowly on country byways and isolated roads.

We immediately discovered that the car had to be started in the conventional manner, depressing the gasoline accelerator, which led to the gasoline line and gas carburetor. Once we were well out of town with a "hot" engine, we could slip the foot over onto the diesel accelerator and the car would purr along at any speed like a sleek cheetah—except when climbing a hill. Then it would roar like a lion in protest against its diesel diet. We soon discovered that we had to simultaneously use the right foot on the gas pedal and the left foot on the diesel pedal to maintain top speed on inclines.

Through embarrassing experimentation we also learned that we had to anticipate stops a quarter-mile ahead of time. If we didn't take the foot off the diesel accelerator then so we could clear the diesel fuel from the fuel line by pumping gasoline into the system, we were enveloped in thick blue smoke when we came to a halt. Unless the diesel line was cleared, the oil remaining in the heating coils would flood the engine compartment under the hood and looked as if the car were on fire.

The blue smoke terrified onlookers, and several times the cloud of smoke was penetrated by a bucket of sand, a squirt of foam or a thorough hosing down. We usually managed to call out, "It's not serious! What with the gas rationing, we've converted to diesel!"

That left them with mouths hanging open.

We perfected the switch from one pedal to the other, and soon were making skilled stops, more or less. We bragged that it cost us very few ration stamps to drive now, and only a half-cent per mile to power our auto on diesel.

The devil was surely tempting us to try the impossible: a trip halfway across the continent, when most citizens were soberly staying at home. But we determined we would take the children to see their aged grandfather in Texas during our summer vacation.

It didn't occur to us to first investigate the availability of diesel fuel along the route we had chosen. Naively, we assumed we'd take "pot luck." As we progressed, our diesel system got used to a variety of grades of fuel, from pure kerosene to much more sophisticated diesel oils. Whatever they had, that's what we were looking for, with no complaints uttered. Prices ranged from 8 to 15 cents per gallon, but our cost remained a steady half-cent per mile for the entire 3,000-mile trip.

Still, our journey could have classified as a comedy of errors. The ultimate disaster occurred a few miles outside Wichita, Kan. The day was extremely hot, and after a stop for a drink of cold juice, we developed a persistent vapor lock in the gas line.

Finally my husband—in a sudden impulse born of his annoyance at the car's refusal to start—poured a bit of his icy drink from the Thermos onto the hot carburetor.

Unfortunately, the cold liquid also fell on the glass filter beside the carburetor, cracking that all-important component.

We attempted to repair the glass reservoir by applying a tourniquet of adhesive tape and a bit of baling wire we found along the road. But gas continued to spurt through.

Finally my husband volunteered to ride the fender with the hood slightly elevated while he gradually poured gasoline from a drinking cup directly into the carburetor. The idea was to keep the gasoline firing so it could warm the diesel until the diesel system could take over.

We started out smoothly enough, but when the "City Limits" sign loomed large, I slowed a bit, causing the car to stutter. Pouring a little more gas into the carburetor, my husband hollered, "Don't slow up for anything!"

I put my head out the window. "What about stop signs?" I yelled.

He called back, "Try hard to anticipate each one of them, so you won't have to come to a complete stop! If you do, we'll smoke and tie up traffic for a mile!" Passersby were already beginning to notice us, some unfavorably.

Smugly I negotiated the first two lights without slowing. At the third light I managed a pause which might have been called a "full stop" under the most lenient interpretation.

Then I swung into a right turn to go around that block, planning to hit the green light during a second pass at the intersection.

For my maneuver, I was rewarded with

"Great thinking, Honey!" from my copilot out there on the fender.

Finally I spotted a downtown garage with a large sign which read "Service Entrance." I sailed right through that open door, squealing my tires with the abrupt turn, and shouting, "Duck, Darling, duck, if you don't want to lose

A photograph of the Oldsmobile that was dieselized for the long trip to Texas. We avoided the use of precious gas ration stamps in the energy crunch of World War II. This was at the start of our trek; I'm pictured with one of our two sons, who is pointing to Air Force planes stunting in the sky above.

your head as our final disaster of the day!"

A bevy of mechanics soon gathered around our smoking car. One wag slapped his thigh and said, "Madam, that's the fanciest radiator ornament I've seen on an Olds. Did you run down your husband and pin him up there as a souvenir?"

They volunteered to repair the strange automobile that had "come all the way from California on a few dollars' worth of diesel fuel." Suddenly they started to outbid each other for its purchase, but we insisted, "No sale!"

Perhaps thanks to some guardian angel who looks after fools and children, that car got its two drivers, their two small sons and a collie dog all the way from California to Texas and back. We arrived home safely, and as sane as anyone could be who would undertake such a journey in the first place! ❖

Water, Water Everywhere!

By Evelyn Lyon

Perhaps it was because we were country people, or perhaps it was because I had a Scottish-Irish mother and a Scottish grandmother, or perhaps it was a sign of the times, but when I was growing up, we wasted nothing—absolutely nothing. Certainly water was one of the main things we conserved.

We were blessed with a good water system. There was a deep well in our back yard where a big iron pump afforded good water. My dad had installed a pitcher pump inside the kitchen, thus bringing "water in the house." It came from a cistern outside the kitchen door; when it rained, water from the eaves filled it. There was also a big rain barrel at the edge of the wash house to catch any rainwater coming off the roof.

In the barn lot there was an enormously deep well. My dad bragged that it was so deep, it could never be pumped dry. It had a big iron pump and a tall squeaky windmill.

It was second nature to conserve water. None was ever thrown out or wasted. Our household tasks and meals were planned carefully to conserve water. When vegetables were washed, the water was carried to the garden or flower bed and poured around the young plants. The water the vegetables were cooked in was used in the gravy or thickened with a little cream to make a delicious sauce. It was never poured down the drain.

Dishwater was always put in the hog feed; Dad felt the suds helped the hogs. Leftover coffee, tea and drinking water from the table was used to water the houseplants.

We had no indoor plumbing, but we did have a sink in the kitchen where we washed our hands. The water from this operation ran out into a bucket underneath; it became water for the chickens, geese and ducks.

We took our baths in a big galvanized washtub. This water was used the next morning to water the garden and flowers in summertime; in winter it was heated on the back of the old black cookstove and was used to warm the chickens' drinking water.

Laundry water really went the rounds. Used first for washing clothes, the sudsy water was next used to scrub kitchen and pantry floors, the porches, and finally the outhouse. Whatever was left found its way to a flower bed, garden or around the base of a tree or shrub.

Water caught in the rain barrel was special—it was soft. We used it to wash hair, silk hose and delicate laundry, in that order. Whatever was left was used for small cleaning jobs—windowsills, cabinet fronts, kitchen chairs, table legs and porch railings. Mother was a meticulous housekeeper and scrubbing was one of her greatest virtues.

Years have come and gone. I have moved away from the little farm, but the conservative values of my youth linger. I find it very difficult to turn on the faucet and just "let the water run," or see gallons gush through a lawn hose, or hear it gurgle through an automatic washer and on down into the sewer. I'm sure there is no way we can go back to the good old days, and certainly modern conveniences have brought us great comfort, but my thrifty upbringing compels me to have great respect for water.

In our age it is very important that we make the most of our natural resources and energy. All it takes is a little attention and deliberate action. Perhaps it would be good for us to try the "conservative tricks" of our ancestors. ❖

Paper Recycling the Way It Was

By Mary Kentra

Recycling is a word I wouldn't have recognized when I was a kid in the early 1900s, yet its practice was part of my life. Take paper, for instance. We didn't subscribe to a newspaper, because we couldn't afford it, but Papa brought old ones home from the restaurant where he worked. Here are a few of the ways we managed to use it.

First, Papa read it religiously, to translate the news later for his Slav friends who weren't as fluent in English.

Then Mama labored over the "funnies," learning to read aloud as part of her citizenship course.

Then we four kids fought over the color Sunday edition of The Katzenjammer Kids, Mutt and Jeff, and Jiggs. Our American Aunt Lizzie courageously rescued the remains and sewed them together, binding the backs with strips from old sheets, "so you kids will have them to read this winter when you can't go out." (Too bad she didn't patent the idea; it preceded kids' comic books by 50 years!)

What was left of the newspaper was stacked carefully in the basement for various household uses, from midwifery to beauty aids.

The cleanest section made shelf paper for the food and dish pantry, with the bottoms cut in intricate designs that folded over the shelves "to look pretty."

Sister Anne, who was taking dressmaking in high school, swiped whatever portion she could to make patterns. She would lay old dresses, skirts, aprons or nightgowns on the kitchen table and cut the desired pattern from newspaper. Only then would Ma or the high-school sewing teacher trust her to cut into purchased fabric, or whatever usable parts were left

of Ma's or our adult aunties' discarded clothes.

The younger children fought over pages to make covers for textbooks we purchased at the beginning of the term and sold to the next class (if we were fortunate enough to get promoted before the books were worn and soiled).

Ma's housekeeping methods demanded a huge supply of old newspapers. Vinegar and water were combined for window washing, and crumpled newspapers dried the panes.

When she swept her two precious wedding-present carpets, Ma would dunk newspapers in a pail of water. She'd make small wads of damp paper and scatter them around the room to "eat the dust" that the broom raised. This also saved her curtains from getting soiled.

When a window broke and family finances didn't permit immediate repair, several thicknesses of newspapers were pasted over the hole using a glue made of egg whites.

In rainy weather, thick layers of newspaper at the front and back entries to the house absorbed some of the mud and moisture before the children tracked it all into the house.

And when a midwife was due to perform her duties, she arrived several days early and sewed inch-thick pads of newspapers between old pillowcases and baked them for hours in the oven of the wood-burning stove until they were "fit to be used in the delivery bed." Even the baby, after her arrival, was entitled to her share of yesterday's news, which was folded in pads under her diaper to absorb any overflow.

In the winter, the older children and adults laid layers of newspaper between the springs and mattresses of their beds to keep the bed warmer. The kitchen stove just couldn't heat all the house. Mama was eternally warning us, "Don't waste a scrap of paper; we need some to start the wood fire in the kitchen stove."

In the summertime, the ends of newspapers were cut in fringe and hung on a line over the kitchen table, so that the cut ends would sway in the breeze and keep flies off the food.

It's no wonder that big sister had to hide some pages of old papers in her bedroom closet so she'd have them to tear into strips to wind her hair around when she wanted tight curls for a special party.

Other paper was just as precious and useful as news print. Old Sears and Montgomery Ward catalogs were treasured playthings in winter. In a household where purchased toys were unknown, cutouts of the advertised merchandise were contrived into ingenious playthings.

Even the baby was entitled to her share of yesterday's news, which was folded in pads under her diaper at bedtime to absorb any overflow.

We cut out the models and used them for paper dolls. "Playing store" with unlimited merchandise cut from catalogs was a favorite winter pastime, with the pictures stored in shoe boxes to use over again and again.

When a grocer put fruit or vegetables in a bag, it was carefully stored for the boarders' lunch. If they were careful, the mustard- and ketchup-stained bags could travel back and forth to the shipyards for several weeks.

And catalogs provided entertaining reading (and other useful functions) in the outhouse. When an "inside toilet" was added to our house, the bathroom boasted a cloth pocket heaped with tissue squares provided by the grocer. He saved them for his favorite customers after removing them from the oranges he sold.

Shoe boxes and other cardboard provided innersoles for children's shoes when they wore out before there was enough money to go to the shoe repairman or buy new ones.

In later years, the rags-bottles-and-sacks man carted away newspapers and other discards in his horse-drawn wagon. Then another war and the emergence of an affluent society, paper napkins, paper towels, disposable diapers and other throwaways came on the scene.

Now the cycle is complete, with a return to "ecology." But I've known about it for more than half a century—only during my childhood, it was called "economy." ❖

John Slobodnik

Pages From My Life

By Florencie Bryant

Feb. 14, 1938—what a date to remember! I was a tiny tot in a red velvet dress, long brown stockings, and black patent leather shoes with ankle straps.

Almost every night for a week or so before the 14th, Mama and my two older sisters and brother sat around the kitchen table after chores, and by the soft yellow light of the kerosene lamp, we cut and pasted, trimmed and ruffled.

Mama always saved her outdated seed catalogs, and Sister would cut out pictures of scarlet zinnias, purple petunias and golden marigolds. Brother cut out colored paper booklets, and if I was very, very careful, I could have the privilege of pasting a beautiful picture of sky blue delphiniums on the front cover.

One sister was very witty, and the charming verses would flow from her pen in an unending flourish, one valentine after another.

Artistic valentines looked back at us with sporty yarn borders and bows, weaving baskets of pink dahlias and snowy candytuft. Teacher's valentine was the best of the lot, truly beautiful, presenting shasta daisies cascading onto a bed of fiery red poppies in the shape of a basket. The verse was neatly signed with love, and red satin ribbon was carefully wound through the handle of the basket.

Feb. 14 was an exciting date in my life. Mama stirred up fudge and peanut brittle, and sometimes candy apples and popcorn balls for me to take to school. Our valentines were wrapped in brown paper and the goodies were bagged up for the long, 2-mile walk to school through snow and unplowed roads.

What an exciting day for a little tot like me! Teacher always gave us store-bought valentines, along with apples and suckers. All the children had high hopes of being chosen to deliver the mail. Those chosen marched up and down the aisles handing out valentines from the big red and white decorated box that stood in the front of our one-room country school.

Teacher opened her valentines to a very hushed class, one after another, holding them up to show us all and telling the name of the giver. We would clap with pleasure, seeing the red flush on the sender's cheeks. Teacher made each and every child feel so very special, and that his or her valentine was the most wonderful!

Artistic valentines looked back at us with yarn borders and bows, weaving baskets of pink dahlias and snowy candytuft.

The excitement stirred us long after the party was over. We were so full of love and joy that the long, cold walk home seemed short. I could hardly wait to get home and show Mama my valentines and share my treats from school.

There was always a surprise from Mama on the big old table when we got home. It was a gift from her loving hands and heart—a tall, heart-shaped cake iced with fluffy pink and white frosting and nestled in a whiskery bed of coconut. Our old blue Dutch pitcher was filled with tangy lemonade, and there were platters full of big molasses cookies, frosted in pink, yellow and white and decorated with hard little red candies. Delicious smells wafted from the iron kettle on the stove, and from the odd pots and pans in the warming oven.

Whenever I feel lost, forlorn, perhaps forgotten, I push aside the curtain of time. Then I can step back again into the past—back to Valentine's Day years ago—and taste cake and cookies, sitting at the supper table, Mama holding her valentine, a halo of lamplight shining on her chestnut hair. ❖

Hand-Me-Downs

Nowadays we hear a lot about the benefits of recycling. I think that's great! Still, recycling and conservation is nothing new to those of us who remember the good old days. Part of using it up meant handing it down, whether to younger siblings, cousins or just neighbors on the next farm.

Janice and I were raised in families which didn't just believe in hand-me-downs—we lived the hand-me-down way of life.

My mother was a seamstress extraordinaire. She could work magic with needle and thread, whether by hand or with the old treadle ma-chine. That was the earliest contact I had with the world of mechanized sewing. I was fascinated by the foot treadle and how a pump on it could move a thrusting needle all the way on top.

One poignant memory of hand-me-downs stands out when I think of Mama and all the work she put in to make sure her children had decent clothes to wear.

The small country school I attended my first eight years was nothing to compare with the high school in which I found myself for my freshman year. *Eighteen kids in a class!* I thought. *And they're all my age!* Actually, I was the youngest in the class. Mama and Daddy had acquiesced to my pleas to start school a year early, so I was only 13 as I entered high school.

For Christmas that year Mama made me one of the best corduroy coats I had ever seen. Where she got the fabric, I will never know. It probably came from an uncle's hand-me-down. She put dozens of hours pulling the old garment apart, fretting with how to make every square inch count. I was small for my age, so I guess that made it a little easier for her.

I couldn't have been prouder when I opened my gift Christmas morning. Never had anyone worn such a grand coat! I wore it all that day, even when Daddy stoked up the wood stove to the melting point. I even slept with it that night, as I usually did with new things, be they puppies, pencils or pocket knives.

With the same pride I wore my new coat to school the first day after Christmas break. One of the older boys noted it and asked where my folks had bought it.

"They didn't buy it!" I fairly busted with pride. "My mama made it for me!"

"Made it!" he exclaimed. "Probably from some old hand-me-down rag! Store bought's a whole lot better than that'll ever be!"

Laughter from the other boys rang down the hall and reddened my cheeks. I slipped off my new coat and hung it up as I hung my head down. It was my first real contact with this city kind of social pressure.

Through the morning hours I worried about how I would be able to sneak out the coat without feeling the sting of more ridicule. By lunchtime, however, my shame had been replaced by a more noble emotion.

I was mad.

When the lunch bell rang, I marched straight to the clothes rack and retrieved my coat. Then I marched straight to the older boy who had made fun of it.

"You're just jealous because you ain't got a coat this nice!" I spit out. "Your mama probably couldn't make something like this if she tried."

After I got up off the floor, I ate lunch. Then I wore my coat proudly back to the classroom and hung it on the back of my seat the rest of the day.

By the next year a growth spurt had robbed me of my corduroy coat. I smiled each time I saw a younger cousin wearing it, however. Thanks to that coat I had learned an important lesson about life, love, pride and the good old days value of hand-me-downs.

—Ken Tate, Editor

Handing Down With Grace

By Helen Colwell Oakley

My, my! Cute as a bug's ear! Too beautiful for words!" gushed the neighbor lady as Mom showed her the little sheer white dresses she had just finished sewing for my sister, Fran, and me. Mom had made them from a lovely white dress that she had had for best for quite a few years.

No one would have ever guessed that the little dresses had been made from a hand-me-down. That's right—Mom couldn't wear the dress any more as it was too tight, so she handed it down to us. We were delighted with the results.

First she opened all the seams and the hem and removed the lace trim. Then she soaked and gently washed the pieces; there was one long piece that had been the skirt with tiny pleats all around it. Mom hung the fabric in the sunshine; this would bleach it, and the breezes would make it fresh and soft again.

Later, in the afternoon, Mom cleared the table and got out her big cutting shears and searched through her pattern box. She cut the two dresses from one pattern by "adjusting" them to us, she said. She'd cut awhile and then hold the pieces up to us. That wasn't so bad, but the pins she used were always pricking us.

Perhaps it was because my first encounter turned out to be such a joyful experience that I never shuddered with distaste when I heard the words "hand-me-down."

After Mom began sewing, my sister and I were so impatient for her to finish that we played with the baby so he would be quiet, and picked up the toys and put them away so Mom could keep working on our dresses.

Finally the dresses were hemmed and ready to try on. They were dainty and beautiful, with lace-edged ruffles all over the bodice and pink satin ribbons on the shoulders. The dresses had 4-inch hems; Mom said they could be let down as we grew taller.

My sister and I couldn't have been prouder of the dresses if they had been brand-new from the catalog or the department store in the city. Everyone admired them, and we were proud as peacocks when Mom would let us wear them for "dress-up."

Perhaps it was because my first encounter turned out to be such a happy, joyful experience that I never shuddered with distaste when I heard the words "hand-me-down."

One day in fifth grade, my girlfriend came to school wearing a very attractive rust-colored coat (an orange shade, very popular in the '30s) trimmed with a luxurious fur collar. "That coat is so pretty, Maria," we chorused as she came to school that day.

"I hate it!" she replied. "It used to be my big sister's, and now my mother says I have to wear it. It's a hand-me-down, so I can't stand it."

Some of the girls sympathized with her, but I told her that she was being silly. The coat looked so pretty on her, it shouldn't matter that it was a hand-me-down. Besides, most people would never know that she hadn't gotten it new from a store.

As one of the older children in my family I did not inherit hand-me-downs from my brothers and sisters. But I did get them from cousins, aunts, friends and neighbors. Mom always freshened up the hand-me-downs, sometimes changing buttons or putting in pleats or putting in a new hem.

I was always thrilled to have something different to wear to school. Once the hired girl gave me a pink fuzzy sweater that had shrunk when she washed it; was I ever a hit that day at school! It had been quite expensive, and no one guessed that it was a hand-me-down—until I spilled the beans!

Perhaps it was because I had no older brothers or sisters who got everything brand-new and then passed it on to me when it was half-worn; but I never understood all the fuss about hand-me-downs, or why it was shameful to wear something someone else had worn. So long as it was clean and looked nice, that was all that mattered to me.

But I had girlfriends who thought it was sinful to wear hand-me-downs. Some of the girls felt better about their hand-me-downs when the teacher confided that she was wearing a dress that had been her sister's. She always dressed so beautifully that we found it very hard to believe that she would ever wear someone else's clothes!

"I told you so! Hand-me-downs are not a disgrace!" I said. "I don't mind wearing them one bit!"

Mom used to tell about letting a hem down one year for one of my sisters, and then putting it back up in another year or two for one of the younger girls, and then letting it down again as my younger sister got taller.

The skirt had been mine in the beginning—after it was made over from one of Mom's. This happened quite often, as families were thrifty and made do in those times.

Nothing was thrown out—grown-ups' coats and suits were cut down to make "new" outfits from unworn pieces of fabric. I remember a coat with a fur collar, and a legging set with a hat to match; all three pieces came from a coat that had been worn for a good many years by a grandfather.

Now here we are today—the practice of hand-me-downs seems to be revolving once again. Many families are passing down outgrown garments which can be worn by younger cousins, friends and neighbors. This means a great savings to parents with several children to clothe; clothing can be very expensive! The giver feels good, as he is doing someone a good turn and cleaning out his closets at the same time.

How about changing hand-me-downs to hand-me-ups? ❖

The Worth of Mama's Quilt

By Ella Kiefer

My aunt was a thrifty lady, and as everyone did then, she made quilts for the family. At the time she made a special quilt, she was an elderly widow living alone and some distance from her family. Back then, 50 miles was quite a distance if you didn't have a car—and where we lived, few people did.

She knew she would not live many more years. She wanted to know that her youngest son would get the money she had saved for him. Her daughters were well taken care of by their husbands, she reasoned, so she felt the money should go to Robert. But how to send it?

Robert and Carolyn were young. The money would seem like a small fortune to them. She thought of just putting it in an envelope and placing it in the folds of the quilt, but she feared it might be lost.

> *Her daughters were well taken care of by their husbands, she reasoned, so she felt the money should go to Robert. But how to send it?*

In time, her daughter Evelyn and her husband came by on their way to visit his parents. Yes, they said, they would take the quilt to Robert and Carolyn. Nothing was said about the money.

Robert was glad to see his sister and he and Carolyn were happy to get the quilt. A short letter was pinned to the quilt, and after Evelyn and her husband left, Robert and Carolyn read it together:

"Dear Robert and Carolyn,

"So sorry I am not able to come visit. Evelyn wanted me to come, but I'm not feeling well enough for the trip.

"This quilt is one of the prettiest I've made and I wanted you to have it. Evelyn said she'd bring it to you.

"If you are ever in need, look to the quilt.

"Love, Mama."

The last line of the letter puzzled Robert and Carolyn. They finally decided that Mama must have meant they were to sell the quilt if they were ever in great need.

Several years passed. The Great Depression was at its worst. Farm produce sold for little; eggs went for 4 cents a dozen—if a buyer could be found. Money was scarce, work was scarce, and when there was work, a man often had to wait for his money.

The pasture was dry and brittle; the cow was dry, the horses little more than bags of bones. Robert watched them from the kitchen window, then turned away, sick at heart. Even the chickens were skinny, hardly worth plucking.

At the edge of the woods he saw the sow and her little ones foraging for acorns. At least they could find something to eat. The family would have fat meat this winter and little else.

The children were also sick. Robert sat on the bed, trying to comfort Robbie. He idly touched the pieces of the quilt—a scrap from Mama's dress, chambray from Dad's shirt, rosy red pieces from his sister's dress. "Rosie in the rosy red dress," they'd teasingly called her.

He felt the urge to look for something, but he didn't know what. A shoe box on the closet shelf caught his eye, so he took the box over to the bed and looked at its contents—old pictures of him and Carolyn, Mama and Dad, Evelyn and Emma, Harold and Rosie. He put the pictures back, pushing aside old letters and receipts. He pulled a folded piece of paper from the bottom of the box. It was a letter from his mother, the one she had sent with the quilt.

"Look to the quilt." The words jumped out at him. He looked at the quilt, faded from washing, the fabric worn in spots. It wouldn't sell now, even if there were someone with money to buy it. He ran his hand over it again, stopping on the rose-red fabric. He felt the material, then felt the next piece, then the red again.

He called Carolyn to ask where the scissors were. Then he carefully snipped the threads and felt under the cotton batting. He pulled out a green folded square that unfolded into a $20 bill. He looked for more; another red square yielded another bill. He felt for more, then stopped. Forty dollars would do a lot; if they needed more, well, the quilt was still there. If there was more money, it would be there too.

He called Carolyn into the bedroom and told her what he had found. She cried quietly, then kissed him when he went out to hitch the thin old horse to the wagon. Blessing her mother-in-law, she sewed the quilt squares back in place.

Robbie still had whooping cough, but that night they ate well and the cattle had a small ration of feed.

One other time, they went to the quilt to pay their bills and put food on the table. After Robert died, Carolyn kept the quilt, though by then it was thin and worn.

Then one day she felt the hard square in the corner. The bill was creased, the fold marks faded from the many washings it had been through. Carolyn went over the quilt carefully in case they'd missed a bill over the years, but that was the last money the quilt held. This Carolyn saved, for who knew when the wolf would knock on the door again? ❖

The Old Rag Carpet

By Ronald T. MacLaren

The rag carpet of yore,
That covered our floor,
Was a wonderful thing to behold.
Not since, nor before,
In shop or in store,
Was a treasure like this ever sold.

Every tint, every hue,
Red, yellow and blue—
It was truly a colorful treat.
Quite gaudy, it's true,
When the carpet was new—
A rainbow of colors complete.

This carpet we had
Was not just a fad,
But was born of necessity's call.
Each lass and each lad,
Even Mother and Dad,
Was a part of that rug in the hall.

Each carpet we laid
Was woven or made
From the shirts and the dresses we wore.
Although tattered and frayed,
Each article played
A part in the rug on the floor.

Every scrap, every mite,
Was stored away tight
In a carpet bag hung on the wall,
And, oh, what a delight,
On a cold winter night,
To sew on a big carpet ball.

When the rags had been wound,
A weaver came 'round,
To finish the job on his loom.
Then the carpet was bound,
And soon could be found
On the floor of the old living room.

With its tints and its stains,
Its colorful chains,
That gave it the stripes aft and fore,
We were paid for our pains,
And could now entertain,
With a dandy new rug on the floor.

In the hall, on the stair,
On the floors everywhere,
Were carpets—the best in the land;
No rugs could compare
With that article rare,
That rag carpet woven by hand.

Some folk that I know,
In that long, long ago,
Preferred that their floors should be bare;
But when the winds blow,
And the firesides glow,
Our family was all gathered there.

From the place they filed,
I've sometimes beguiled
Those treasures from memory's store—
Of the days when a child,
The whole family smiled
From a place in the rug on the floor.

Your Old Kit Bag

By Adeline Minnich

A familiar refrain caught my ear. The commercial lyrics coming from the radio paraphrased a tune from my childhood: "Pack up your troubles in your old Glad Bag, and smile, smile, smile!"

I hummed along, my memory triggered by the old favorite which had been popular during and after World War I. However, Glad Bags are a far cry from kit bags!

In 1918 Mama had no need for Glad Bags. She had no garbage can, no garbage man, no disposal and no trash compactor. Mama managed to have very little rubbish. There was a wastebasket under the sink. As papers accumulated, Papa would burn them on a blackened, ash-covered spot in the vacant lot next door to our home in the northern Ohio steel-mill town of Lorain.

Newspapers and magazines were never burned. They were saved and bundled for the twice-yearly visits from the rag man who clopped around in his horse-drawn cart. He bought Mama's accumulated papers and rags.

My brother Donald and I scoured the neighborhood when the rag man was due because he'd give us a few mighty welcome coins for all the junk we could collect. He weighed everything on hand scales, but Mama had her own scales. If she thought he might be short-changing us, she dragged her own scales out to settle the matter.

Waxed-paper wrappings were smoothed out, folded carefully and stowed in a drawer to be used again to wrap Papa's sandwiches. There were no bottles or glass jars which were not washed and reused for the jam, jelly, ketchup and chili sauce Mama put up every summer.

I can't remember many tin cans, since we ate home-canned fruits and vegetables. Once in a while we had a tin of salmon or tuna. I can't figure out what use Mama made of these cans, but I know she used them for something.

She wasted nothing. "Waste not, want not. Willful waste makes woeful want," she said.

As for all those big brown supermarket bags that pile up in our kitchens today since they're far too good to be thrown away, well, they simply didn't exist. We shopped often, running to the store for Mama to buy fresh meat for supper and maybe a pound of sugar. These items were wrapped in brown paper packages tied up with string, and we carried them home without benefit of a big double-strength bag.

The milkman's horse clip-clopped along early every morning as the milkman hand-delivered our order.

Mama saved every piece of string, winding it onto a fat ball. It was mighty handy for sewing up roasting chickens or flying the kites my brother made every spring from newspaper and flour-and-water paste.

We didn't have wrappings from bread or rolls or fruit, as a bread man came around every day, clanging a bell to alert Mama to run out into the street to select some goodies from his heavenly smelling wares.

The milkman's horse clip-clopped along early every morning as the milkman hand-delivered our order. If Mama was having company and wanted something special, like cottage cheese or cream, she left a note for the milkman in the glass bottle.

None of these door-to-door merchants used paper bags, so we had none to dispose of. Large quantities of fruit came in bushel baskets which we returned to the seller. We kept the bread in a large tin box with a tight hinged lid. Our tea and coffee came right to our door, too, sold by the Jewel Tea Company which gave away coupons and premiums—and Mama saved every one.

I wonder if she could find anything to do with a Glad Bag that would make her "smile, smile, smile"? ❖

A Lesson In Humility

By Clyde J. DeVaux

Growing up there were four children in my family—my sister, Gertrude, 16; my brothers, Frank, 14, and Charles, 10; and I was 8. Our father was the well-respected neighborhood country doctor.

We lived among mostly foreign-born people—Polish, French and German immigrants, most of whom could neither read nor write, and who spoke very poor English. They were laborers in the Pennsylvania Railroad repair shops where they repaired, repainted or scrapped boxcars and passenger coaches. Many of these workmen hauled home the scrap lumber for fuel, and used larger pieces to build outbuildings and even houses.

They had big families and did everything they could to provide for their children. They all made gardens and canned fruit and other produce. They "made over" their older children's clothes to hand down to the younger ones, so patched clothing was a common sight.

My brothers and I were the envy of the other schoolchildren. We had good clothing, a bicycle, skates, sleds, and each of us received an allowance.

My brothers and I were the envy of the other schoolchildren. We had good clothing, a bicycle, skates and sleds, and each of us received an allowance. The others had homemade sleds, and then only one for the family. Some of the children would search the junkyard for cast-off skates. They made their baseballs by winding string around a rubber ball, and used a club or old ax handle for a bat. Most had no ball glove and would catch bare-handed.

They liked to play ball at our house because we had boughten balls, bats, a catcher's mitt and ball gloves, which we shared with everyone. We also had our own ball diamond, on a 5-acre common next to our house. The big boys had made the common ground into a ballpark, but they used it only on Sundays. That left it for us to use on weekdays.

Charles and I received an allowance of 10 cents each. Frank and Gertrude received 25 cents. Each day we stopped at the grocery store where we would buy some of the smaller candies—red-hots, licorice babies or mixed candy. We did this so we could share it with other children who got candy only once a month, when their parents paid their grocery bills. Then the grocer would give them a treat of 2 pounds of mixed candy. With families of eight children or more, however, 2 pounds didn't go very far. So we always had boys in line for a small helping of our candy.

Sometimes we bought bananas or apples instead. Apples were 35 to 50 cents per bushel, and bananas cost 10 cents a dozen.

Because of all this, we were pampered by all the other boys and were admired by all the girls in our classes.

I often brought my teacher flowers from our garden, or an apple or a banana. It was whispered that I was the teacher's pet, and so I was.

My teacher was a very pretty young woman who was one of my father's patients. She frequently gave me a note to take to my father for medicine which I would bring to her the following day.

Most of the other children never got enough to eat at home. Their parents doled out the food, and there were no second helpings. When I had an apple, one of them would always ask me for the core, and he'd eat everything but the seeds. I always left a little more on the core than I would have if I'd just intended to throw it away.

If I had a banana, someone would ask me for the peel and then scrape the inside with his teeth. I always left part of the banana so he would at least get a taste. They'd even accept gum after I'd chewed all the flavor out!

As soon as weather permitted, all the poorer children—boys and girls—would go barefoot to save their shoes. I think Emma and I were the only ones in our classroom who continued to wear shoes during the warmer weather.

It was near the end of the school year and children had been going barefoot for weeks. It was the custom to have a little exercise to which all the parents were invited so they could watch their children perform. Ours was a simple march. The teacher selected children of equal size to march side by side. My partner was not only from the poorest family, but also the dirtiest. Clyde Hook had no Sunday clothes, and was barefoot. I felt I would be belittled by marching beside that dirty, ragged boy.

I stayed after school and asked my teacher to give me a better-dressed partner. When she asked me why, I told her that I thought we would both look out of place, with me wearing my best clothing and him wearing only his school clothes and being barefooted. She smiled and said she would see what she could do.

Then she happened to see my father—and she told him about my request! She thought it was cute, but my father did not. His own father had died when he was only 7 years old, and he knew what poverty was. My father had worked his way through college and knew too well what it meant to be constantly in need.

That evening he called me into his office and asked me why I didn't want to march with Clyde Hook. I explained that he had no good clothes and would be barefooted.

"Who buys his clothes?" Father asked.

"His parents," I replied.

"Who buys yours?"

"Mom does, but you give her the money," I answered.

"Now if George Hook was your father, who would buy your clothes?"

"He or Mrs. Hook, but in that case, I would never get a new suit, because he only gets the clothes his older brother outgrows," I told him.

"Then you wouldn't have any better clothes than he has, nor would you have shoes. Isn't that right?"

Father continued, "Now let's see what each of you has done or possessed by your own efforts. Can you spell better than he?"

"No," I replied.

"How about arithmetic, geography, English, art—are you better in any of these than he?"

"Yes, I am better in art than anybody in the whole class," I proudly replied.

"But not better than he in other subjects?"

"No, only in art," I replied.

"Then, you see, he has more to be proud of than you. What he has, he did himself. What you have is one subject and what I have given you. You are proud of something you have not done for yourself, but for what I have provided. You send that boy to me and I will see that he has both good clothing and shoes."

I was glad to see Clyde get a new suit and shoes. I couldn't wait to tell him.

When the day for the program arrived, I couldn't find my clothes or shoes.

"Where are my clothes and shoes?" I called down to Mother.

"Aren't they in your closet?" she called back.

"No, there is nothing here," I answered.

"Oh! I remember now. Your father took them to the dry cleaners and your shoes to be repaired. I guess he forgot to go after them. You know how busy he is. Just shine your old shoes and wear your school clothes. Nobody has anything better to wear."

I had no choice. There was no time to go the 2 miles into town to the cleaners, and I wasn't sure where he had taken my shoes.

Mother went with me to the school party. I was still to march beside Clyde Hook. When he appeared, to my surprise he had a new suit and shoes. Father had gotten him a whole new outfit. Clyde had even washed his hands and face real well, which was unusual for him. Everybody commented on how nice he looked. Now I was the one who had to march with a boy better dressed than I was. I felt really embarrassed.

That evening while we were having supper, Clyde Hook appeared at the door, carrying a suit box. When he entered the room, I saw that he was also carrying a pair of shoes.

Then I understood. Clyde had worn my suit. Father had turned the tables on me by loaning my clothes to Clyde—and letting me find out how it felt to be in the other boy's shoes.

I did not resent what my father had done. I appreciated what he provided for me, but as he had explained, I was taking credit for it, even though I was entirely dependent on him.

In reality, Clyde Hook had far more than I did. He studied hard because there was nothing else for him to do. My bicycle and many toys occupied too much of my time. Thanks to this lesson from my father, I studied harder and got better grades.

I never had to wear my older brother's clothes which he had outgrown, even though they were still good. They were just the right size for Clyde Hook, as were Charles' shoes. From then on, Mother gave Clyde Charles' outgrown suits and shoes. She even had the shoes repaired before she sent them.

This had another good effect: With better clothes to wear, Clyde began to clean up more. When the next party came along, I was glad to have him as a marching partner.

I never forgot that lesson in humility. Had my father simply scolded me, I would have forgotten all about it. It was a lesson I never forgot for the rest of my life.

The strangest thing happened after I became a grandfather. My daughter and her husband are both college graduates. They have a beautiful home and plenty of money. When my granddaughter was 10 years old, she mentioned that she wasn't inviting a certain girl to her house because her parents were poor.

"Is she a nice girl?" I asked.

"Yes, she's nice," she replied, "but she doesn't have nice clothes."

"Are they dirty? Doesn't she have clean hands and face?"

"She is clean and her clothes are too, but they're homemade," my granddaughter replied.

I then went back to the same questions my father had asked me back in 1908, when I had the same ideas. When I got through with her, she saw the situation in a different light. The example my father had set again served a corrective purpose. I am sure that one day my granddaughter will use it on her children, should the situation arise. ❖

> *"He has more to be proud of than you. What he has, he did himself. You send that boy to me and I will see that he has both good clothing and shoes."*

Just One Pair of Shoes

By Minnie Christine Blythe

When I see all my children's and grandchildren's shoes lined up in their closets or, worse still, scattered around every which way, I think of my one pair of black shoes. Count them—just two shoes!

When I was a child on the farm in Idaho, I had very few things: two shoes, two stockings and two dresses—one Sunday-go-to-meeting dress, and one school dress, which was laundered every weekend to wear again for another week.

I remember the old joke about the girl trying to impress her boyfriend. As she was going up the stairs, she called out to her mother so that he could hear: "Ma, which dress shall I wear, the red one or the blue or the brown or the green?"

"Wear the green one, you fool," her mother called back. "That's the only one you have!"

To this day, if I have two of anything—toasters, waffle irons, coffeepots, you name it—I feel I should give one away; that it's a sin to own two of anything, especially if someone needs the other. After all, I can only use one!

But to get back to those black shoes …

I was youngest, so I often wore shoes that were too large for me until I grew into them.

they were sturdy for trudging the dirt roads to school, or cutting across fields if in a hurry. They were high-top button shoes, worn all week to school and then polished on Saturday nights for church. Black shoes were so common that even after my sister acquired a pair of brown shoes, she continued to ask, "Where's the brown shoe blacking?"

We wore these shoes until we could wear them no more—not that they ever wore out. They must have eventually worn out, but I don't recall it. By then we had outgrown them and they had been handed down to the next child.

I was youngest, so I often wore shoes that were too large for me until I grew into them. Fortunately, I suffered no negative aftereffects except misshapen toenails. I can still walk a few miles at age 79.

Of course in summer—glorious summer!—we could go barefoot. We could hardly wait for the snow to melt so we could take off those horrible, black, ribbed stockings. (All stockings were black and ribbed—I wonder why?)

How we reveled in free feet after a winter of stockings, shoes, overshoes and leggings (I believe the English call them "spats"). I wonder if they are still worn in cold countries, or if something better has replaced them.

We had one hat for Sundays and one homemade bonnet for weekdays. We rarely showed our faces to the sun. Now we know too much exposure to the sun can be harmful.

Then there was the long-handled underwear! The long legs reached down to our ankles. It took some doing to fold them at the bottoms and pull our long stockings up over them, but we became experts at an early age. The long sleeves reached the wrists. No one I knew wore short sleeves.

I remember going alone to a public dance. It was perfectly safe in those days. The dances were supervised, and no one who had drunk or was drinking was allowed on the floor. A floor walker introduced us to different partners.

I was wearing my only coat. (Although I was grown and working away from home, I still thought one coat was enough. No one I knew owned more than one.) We put our coats in the cloakroom. No one was there to supervise it; the coats were stacked on shelves, and after the dance we each found our own—if we could!

I arrived in the cloakroom just as a girl wearing my coat was going out the door. I grabbed her by the coattail. "Come back here!" I screamed. "You are wearing my coat!"

Fortunately I had marked it and could identify it. She said not a word; just took it off and handed it to me! I wonder if she came to the dance without a coat, hoping to acquire one!

The worst thing about those black shoes was sitting in school all day with snowmelt squishing in them. It was not unusual at our school.

We walked to school through deep snowdrifts, and the snow sifted over the tops of our shoes and overshoes, sometimes even through our leggings. My shoes never dried completely until I went home at night and emptied the water out of them. Then we dried our feet in front of the fire.

Strangely enough, we had no more sore throats or colds than kids have nowadays. ❖

White Shoes

By Ann Tompert

Every time I wear white shoes, I remember what happened one May more than 60 years ago.

I was in first grade in a Catholic school. For weeks, it seemed, the whole student body had been practicing for the traditional May Procession which would take place in the evening and conclude with the crowning of the Virgin Mary in church.

Then, on the day of the long-awaited event, it was announced that only those girls with white dresses and white shoes would be allowed to march. Disaster! The white dress was no problem, but white shoes? I was a farm child during the Great Depression, and I was lucky to have one pair of sturdy brown oxfords.

But that didn't stop me. When our nun asked how many of us had white shoes, a scattering of hands popped up— and mine was among them. Now, I knew that even if my folks had the money, my father didn't have time to make the 10-mile trip to the nearest town during the busy planting season. Yet, with a child's faith that could move mountains, I was sure I'd be in the May Procession that evening, wearing white shoes.

After school that afternoon, my faith wavered a bit when I announced to my mother that I had to have white shoes, and she said, "I'm not a magician. You'll have to wear the shoes you have, or not go."

I wept and wailed a great deal, I'm afraid, but my mother was not swayed. When my father came in from the fields for supper, I blubbered out my problem to him. After a few minutes of thoughtful silence, he solved it with the resourcefulness typical of pioneers.

Taking a pair of my worn-out black shoes, he painted them white.

My faith was justified. No one in the procession that night marched more proudly than I did. ❖

Mother's Make-Overs

By Berniece Van Dusen

Y ou can't buy such material today," my sister and I used to hear over and over again in those pre-World War I days when clothes were wonderfully made. Our mother made over clothes that had fascinating histories.

We once watched with awe as she ripped apart an overcoat that belonged to Grandfather. As she remarked on its excellent material, out came the lining, as fresh and new on the underside as it must have always been. It became my new spring coat. Mother made me one every year for my birthday, when I passed my own outgrown coat to my little sister, who coveted it.

Once we girls discovered a bonus interlining of new-looking plaid, just the right size for a jacket for our youngest cousin. The original outside may have been the one to which Mother added a fur lining and brand-new astrakhan collar and cuffs.

We thought it was so becoming on our father.

From a box of clothes from a relative who always bought expensive things, I snatched a snowy white beaver hat for my own. But it had a disappointingly pinched-in crown, like an old-fashioned lady's waist. I would have had to hold it on with hat pins.

While I admired it, Mother's shears snipped the crown from the brim. Then she "ruined" the crown by slashing the bottom. I spread these apart and clamped the crown onto my head. Then Mother trimmed the inside of the furry brim. When I put that on too, it looked great!

Mother stitched a strip of buckram to the devastated crown and rejoined it to the brim, covering the operation's scars with wide, white satin ribbon.

I looked exactly the way I wanted to when we took our Sunday seats in church, three rows from the front. But my beautiful new hat was headachy-tight. I suffered, motionless, until every head was bowed.

Then I reached up under the brim and pulled out the large bone hairpin that was causing my misery.

That day's text did not stay in my mind. I am certain, though, that it was not about the wedding guest without the proper raiment.

Another tale about Mother's make-overs concerns a long baby dress with crocheted lace and insertion made from No. 100 sewing thread.

It was prepared for the first baby—me. Later my sister wore it. When we were past babyhood, the tucked lace flounce actually stretched enough to become the bottom ruffles on three little-girl princess slips.

Years later my small daughter wore the lace flounce from my slip until it wore out. Since my sister had no daughters, her slip skipped a generation, only to show up at my house one morning on a tiny great-niece.

Little Mary Kay skipped around my house wearing the very same spiderweb lace and matching insertion that her unknown great-grandmother had crocheted 50 years before. Evidently she had made that lace to endure! ❖

How We Got Our Clothes

By C.W. Henderson

Years and years ago, everybody kept a large gang of sheep. We depended on their wool for most of our clothes. When I was small, Mother had a little knee-high platform where she sheared her sheep. She was an awfully strong woman. I remember seeing her lift a sheep that weighed at least 100 pounds up onto that platform. I don't remember that she ever tied the sheep's legs. She'd just lay it on its side, shear one side, then turn the sheep over and repeat the process.

Mother piled the wool on a large blanket until she got all she could carry. Then she took it into the house and washed it until it was as white as snow.

Once the wool was washed, Mother carded it into little rolls to spin into thread. Mother would put a shuck on the spindle and turn the old spinning wheel. She would draw out a woolen thread 6 or 8 feet long, then wind it back onto the spindle. She repeated this until she'd made a good-sized broach. Then she'd take it off the spindle and put on another shuck to repeat the process.

They somehow managed to get a large hank of cotton thread which Mother called the "chain." She called the woolen thread the "filling."

When I was very small, Mother had an old loom on the north side of the log house up on the hill.

A large shelter was built over the loom, and there Mother would sit, weaving from morning until night.

When she'd woven as far as she could reach, she'd roll the cloth onto a big beam. From this she made our clothes.

Of course, there was no such thing as a sewing machine in our home. Mother had a pair of scissors, a thimble and some needles.

She cut the cloth and made all our clothes by hand. It seemed to me that Mother could just look at us boys and, without any pattern, make clothes to fit us.

What about Father? He certainly didn't lead a "gravy" life. With 10 hungry mouths to fill, Father had to work away from home a great deal—not eight hours a day or 40 hours a week, but from daylight until dark, six days a week, and that for 50 cents a day.

Father made all the shoes we boys wore until we were grown. He dug out a big vat in a large poplar log and tanned his own leather. He made shoe lasts for all the kids. He had us stand on a piece of paper and he drew around our feet to make patterns for the lasts.

Father pegged the bottoms of our shoes with sharpened wooden pegs he made himself from maple blocks. With an awl, he made holes for the pegs, then drove the pegs into the wooden lasts. After the shoe was completed, it was some job to cut the pegs loose and get the last out of the shoe.

Father often worked late into the night. When it was my turn for shoes, I stayed up and held a torch for him so he could see to work.

After we got big enough to hoe our row, Father did not have such a hard time. We went up in the gap of the mountain and cleared two big fields. Father got John Kiser to bring his

Father made all the shoes we boys wore until we were grown. He dug out a big vat in a large poplar log and tanned his own leather.

steer and lay off the corn ground. We planted our corn, and that was the only time all during that summer that there was a plow in the field. We all had hoes and kept the bushes cut down all summer. The cove land was fertile and we began to grow a fine chance of corn.

Little heifer calves were selling very cheap, and our folks bought three. In the course of a couple of years, as the old saying goes, we were just swimming in milk, butter and other dairy products.

With plenty of corn for bread and feeding the cows, and with a few garden vegetables thrown in for good measure, we were enjoying some top-notch living.

I reckon we had the best father and mother the Lord ever made! They never sent their children to church and Sunday school—they always took them, and that is much better. It gave us an example we never forgot. Even after children are grown and married with children of their own, they will always pattern their lives after the examples they learned in childhood at the knees of their father and mother. ❖

Quilting Addicts

By Elizabeth R. Sphar

Addicted to quilting? Yes, believe it or not, I belong to the fourth generation of a family of quilting addicts. Three of Great-Grandmother's quilts have been handed down to me, but my memories start with my grandmothers. Both must have been born with needles in their hands, for I seldom saw either when she wasn't piecing or quilting. Their styles of quilting and living differed, but those differences enriched my life.

Grandma Fisher started married life in a sod shanty in South Dakota. She and Grandpa took a big bag of cloth scraps along with a few pieces of furniture, a plow, a few tools and a milk cow tied to the back of the wagon drawn by two mules. Grandma's prize possession was a set of quilting frames her mother gave her as a wedding present. They were made of good, sturdy wood that wouldn't warp or splinter.

> *They must have been born with needles in their hands, for I seldom saw either when she wasn't piecing or quilting.*

Grandma said that if it hadn't been for her scrap bag which she used when she spent her lonely days making quilts, she'd have lost her mind. There was nothing as far as the eye could see, not a house or a tree—only flat land.

Their nearest neighbors were 20 miles away. They visited only once a month unless the men had to help each other with a project. Grandpa was in the fields from sunup till sundown, or away for supplies.

For several years there was no one with whom she could trade scraps and no money for new fabric. She made everyday quilts

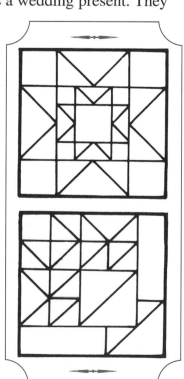

from flour sacks and the good parts of worn-out overalls. Lots of quilts, warm if not decorative, were needed during the below-zero winters.

Within three years Grandpa built a real house; the crops succeeded, Mother was born, and a village grew nearby.

Mother was taught to quilt as soon as she could hold a needle. She taught me just as she had been taught. We lived in town though Dad was a farmer. He drove our Ford out to Grandpa's farm and helped him. Soon, Dad was taking major responsibility and Grandpa was helping.

But Grandma's habits didn't change. She still quilted every day. She liked to piece and quilt alone, except for Mama and me. She said that after those early years alone, a group of cacklin' women made her nervous.

Mama liked to quilt any way, any time. Dad had put up frames in an empty downstairs room which was to be Grandma and Grandpa's if they ever came to live with us. In the meantime, we called it "the quilting room." Three of Mother's Methodist Church friends came every Thursday to quilt. Each brought a potluck dish for lunch.

How I looked forward to "quilting day"! Two of their girls came to play with me. We kept our mothers' needles threaded, five or six pieces. When the women needed more thread they'd call us in from the yard.

Some of the quilts assembled by quilting addicts like me are, facing page, Stars and Squares (top) and Grape Basket. The blocks at right are, top to bottom, Star of Many Points, Tulip in a Vase, Little Red House, Star and Cross and Blazing Star.

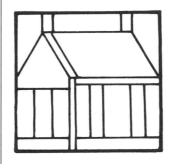

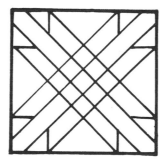

We'd thread their needles, stick them in a row atop the quilt, and run out to play again. Sometimes we'd watch awhile if the quilt was especially colorful or complicated. Sometimes they'd let us quilt awhile if the quilt was an everyday one for one of them.

Several times a year the Methodist Ladies had a big quilting bee at the church. If there was a fire or bad twister in the community, they would have special bees for those who had lost their belongings. Otherwise, they sold some quilts for money for church painting or repairs. Some were sent to missionaries. Each new bride from the church was given a quilt. Quilts were always needed for something or other.

Friends were valued and needed in pioneer days, so Friendship Quilts were popular. The recipient would decide on a motif—perhaps a rose quilt. As many as 12 friends would each piece a block, and often sign her name on it with quilting thread or embroidery floss. Then they'd have a "friendship bee," sew the blocks together and quilt them along with pleasant reminiscences. Popular rose designs were Bud and Rose Wreath, Wreath of Roses, Whig Rose, Wild Rose and personalized versions of them.

Grandma liked geometric designs such as Log Cabin, Double Irish Chain (she was part Irish), Straight Furrow, Trip Around the World, and Quilt Trip.

Geometric designs are my favorites, too—easier to make than curved pieces. I made my first quilt when I was 5 or 6; it was just a square block design for my rag doll's bed.

My other Grandma lived in a big white frame house in a small Maryland town. She too was a quilter. I'm sure she had scrap or "piece" bags, as she was a saver and taught me to make use of everything.

But most of her quilts were made from new material, and most were appliquéd.

She also made beautiful crazy quilts from odd-shaped, hit-and-miss pieces. She sewed them onto square block backings. Some were silk and satin, some wool and velvet. Colorful feather-stitching outlined each piece.

Women tried to outdo each other, making as many different patterns of stitches as possible. I liked the crazy quilts best and when I was sick, I'd spend hours studying the stitching patterns to see if any two were alike.

When a grandmother, mother or aunt taught a child to quilt, she taught more than sewing. She taught tradition, family and community history, discipline, cooperation, tolerance, planning and completing a task, and pleasant conversation.

Quilts made from scraps record a family's life, its ups and downs, its relatives and friends. Quilts are personal, made for a member of the family, a close friend, a hoped-for husband. When I look at my quilts, I see Grandma in her Sunday best, Mother at the stove baking or canning, my 16th birthday party, my graduation. There's even a piece of the nightgown I wore when I had the measles. ❖

Grandmother's Fan Quilt Block

Piece A
Cut 5 Fan Sections
from different fabrics

Piece B
Cut 1
solid fabric

Piece together the 5 fan sections, folding seam allowance under. Join this completed section with Piece B.

Finally, appliqué the fan to a 15½" square block (includes ¼" seam allowance).

This completes one 15" block with ¼" seam allowance all around.

The Rag Treasure Bag

By Gertrude R. Lobrot

When I was a child, every home had a rag bag. In it were rags for kite tails and baby-doll dresses, and pieces for cleaning windows and wiping up spilled milk. My grandmother's rag bag was special; no one else's was like hers. She had all the aforementioned things, but much more, too.

In fact, Grandmother had two rag bags. They occupied the bottom shelf of the old-fashioned walnut wardrobe in Grandmother's bedroom. Webster says a rag is "a piece of cloth considered of little or no worth." But Grandmother's rags didn't fit Webster's definition at all. Every piece of cloth, no matter how small, was useful to her. She washed and pressed every piece.

I was happy when Grandmother would say to me, "Gertrude, bring me the big rag bag. I want to cut rag strips to make your mother a new bathroom rug." I'd dig deep down into the bag and be surprised at the color of the cloth that came up in my hand.

Sometimes it was pink, sometimes blue; that bag held colors of every hue. Grandmother would cut the fabric into 1-inch strips and sew them together end-to-end. Then we rolled them into balls for weaving.

As we worked, Grandmother would tell me whose dress was made from each piece of cloth. She had five girls, and this was interesting to me. I was so excited when I found a piece of cloth from one of my dresses, or Mother's.

Occasionally there would be something of my great-grandmother's, and then Grandmother would tell me how Great-Grandmother had left her family in Scotland and was married at sea by the captain of the ship. Her folks disowned her for leaving her homeland to come to America, and they did not want her to marry Great-Grandfather.

There was a piece of Great-Grandmother's traveling dress in that bag, a Scotch plaid. Every time I brought it out, Grandmother would hold it in her hand, caress it and say, "We won't use it just yet."

Her other treasure bag was a smaller bleached flour sack. When Grandmother used things from this bag, she worked at the large dining-room table. The contents of the bag were special. It contained velvet, colorful satin ribbons, fine lace and embroidered trimmings. These lovely scrap remnants had been given to her by my uncle who had a large dry-goods store.

From the contents of this bag Grandmother fashioned dainty collars for my dresses, ribbons for my hair bows and party dresses, and lace to trim my petticoats.

One Christmas she made a quilt for my doll's bed from colorful velvet scraps stitched together with a lazy-daisy stitch and lined with green satin—all from her wonderful rag treasure bag.

Another time, she surprised me with a blue velvet muff to match the new winter coat my mother had made for me. I loved that muff so much that I wanted to take it to bed with me!

As the years went by, she kept me supplied with dainty satin evening bags, collar and cuff sets for my dresses and lovely rag rugs for my bedroom and bathroom.

Today I have my own rag bag, but it contains only pieces of white cloth suitable for polishing furniture and other cleaning jobs. I wish I had a rag treasure bag to share with my little great-granddaughters. They won't have choice memories of Grandmother's rag bags. ❖

The Original Recycled Sack Dress

By Nancy A. Burcham

Recycling containers isn't a new idea. It's a recycled idea! When I was a child in the 1940s, I wore the original sack dress, recycled from sacks that had contained chicken feed before they contained me! I wasn't fond of the chickens on our little farm. They pecked at me when I gathered their eggs, and they scratched out all the seeds I planted in the garden. But I did appreciate the fact that Dad had to supplement their diet with sacks of chicken feed.

When it was time for more chicken feed, Mother and I went along to the feed store where we wandered up and down the aisles lined with towering cotton sacks of chicken feed. Two colorful sacks supplied enough fabric for a Sunday dress for me.

One day at the feed store, I chose a feed sack with red flowers on blue. Mother agreed with my choice and said to the clerk, "I'll need two sacks in the blue background with red rosebuds."

The clerk searched and searched, but she couldn't find a second sack of the same fabric.

"I need two sacks or none," Mother said. "That's how much fabric Grandma has to have to make Nancy's Sunday dress."

I joined in the search for sack number two. Each of us took an aisle and looked up one side and down the other, but with no luck. We were about to give up when, from two aisles away, the clerk shouted, "I found it!" The sack was squeezed in at the bottom of a stack of 12 feed sacks. Finally we got the sack out—and carried out feed for the chickens and fabric for the child.

When the sacks were empty, Mother ripped out the seams, washed the four pieces of fabric, and ironed out the wrinkles. Meanwhile, Grandma and I browsed through the catalog until we decided on the dress style just right for the feed sack and me.

Then Grandma laid a newspaper out on the floor and carefully cut a pattern to fit me. I don't know how she did it, but she never missed in her measurements.

I soon had a recycled, original sack dress to wear to church until it wore out, or I outgrew it—and it didn't cost an extra cent.

With today's inflation and the increase of litter, a return to fabric sacks might be one solution to alleviate our mounting woes. Large flour sacks of denim or permanent-press sugar sacks wouldn't be added to the garbage heap

When I was a child in the 1940s, I wore the original sack dress, recycled from sacks that had contained chicken feed before they contained me!

when they were empty; they could be recycled into denim jeans and shirts. Sacks of plaid flannel, striped linen or checked cotton could be containers for oatmeal, dry dog food, powdered detergents and powdered milk. Just think how colorful the grocery stores would be!

Some may not agree with my plan for ecology and economy. I'll admit it does have a few drawbacks. Someone in the family would have to enjoy sewing, as my grandmother did. And we would need to buy products in large economy size—or wear miniskirts, minishirts and patchwork designs.

But surely, with some careful planning, we could find a way to overcome the drawbacks of my plan. I was quite proud, you see, of the original recycled sack dress my grandmother made for me. ❖

Flour-Sack Underwear

By Ruth Gettle

When I was a maiden fair
Mama made our underwear.
With five tots and Paw's poor pay,
How could she buy lingerie?

Monograms and fancy stitches
Were not on *our* flour-sack britches …
Panty waists that stood the test
With "Gold Medal" on the chest.

Little pants, the best of all,
With a scene I still recall:
Harvesters were gleaning wheat
Right across the little seat.

Tougher than a grizzly bear
Was our flour-sack underwear …
Plain or fancy, three feet wide,
Stronger than a hippo's hide.

Through the years each Jill and Jack
Wore this sturdy garb of sack.
"Waste not, want not," we soon learned;
"Penny saved, a penny earned."

Bedspreads, curtains, tea towels too;
Tablecloths to name a few.
But the best beyond compare,
Was our flour-sack underwear.

Stretching the Menu

Mama's kitchen was the smallest room in the house, tucked warmly between the living room and the bedroom of our tiny home on a rocky hillside in the Ozark Mountains of southwest Missouri.

We didn't have a dining room; we ate where Mama cooked, baked, sewed—just about everything she did in her busy life.

Just like we made do with one bedroom for a family of five, Mama made do in the kitchen without running water, without a gas stove and without electricity.

Mama was a magician in the kitchen. She could have almost nothing in the house to eat, yet come up with a meal that filled our home with such a delectable aroma that it even could pull us from an exciting game of cowboys and Indians in which we were engaged in the front yard. The wafting of that aroma beckoned us to a simple, but wholesome, meal of beans and salt pork, or potato soup or Mama's "goulash" as she called it—a kettle of leftovers turned into just one more dish.

Corn meal was a staple in Mama's kitchen. With it she made wonderful muffins that were so good with eggs and fried potatoes for breakfast. There was nothing better with the pinto beans we saw so often on the supper table than a big pan of flat corn bread.

My best memory of corn bread, however, was lunch of corn bread and milk.

Grandma Stamps and Uncle Bob lived a few hundred feet from our home, and often one or both of them would join us for lunch. Uncle Bob, a bachelor all his life, had become the man of the house when Grandma was widowed at an early age. It was Uncle Bob who introduced me to corn bread and milk.

"Too blamed hot to eat, Geneva," he said to Mama on a sultry summer afternoon. "Think I'll just have some corn bread and milk."

With that Uncle Bob got about half a glass of fresh cow's milk, cut a chunk of Mama's

thick, warm corn bread and stuff it into the glass. He picked up a spoon as he headed outside to his favorite spot, a big oak tree that graced our front yard.

After a while, I hitched up my overalls the same way Uncle Bob did, picked up my own

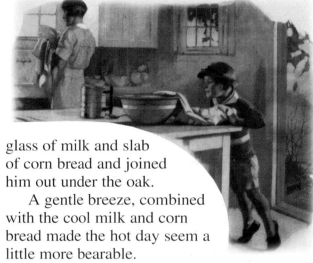

glass of milk and slab of corn bread and joined him out under the oak.

A gentle breeze, combined with the cool milk and corn bread made the hot day seem a little more bearable.

In between spoonfuls of the scrumptious mixture Uncle Bob and I discussed the more important questions of life: Who'll win the World Series this fall? Is it true that June bugs come from grub worms? How come one of the milk cows went dry?

All questions were fielded by Uncle Bob in his earthy manner as we gulped our lunch. "The Yankees will win the Series; don't they always? Yes, June bugs come from grubs, so you gotta get grubs for fishin' before they change. A cow goes dry because … well, maybe you oughta take that one up with your daddy."

I don't think Mama realized how important corn bread and milk was to this country boy. To her it was just a way of stretching the menu in her old-time art of thrift. To me it was summer afternoons of discovery, enrichment and love. It was developing a close lifelong relationship with a special uncle over a glass of milk and corn bread back in the Good Old Days.

—Ken Tate, Editor

Cooking & Canning

By Charles H. Kelly

My mother would have been amazed—and dismayed! Frozen dinners, pizza, fast food, deep-fried chicken, crunchy fish and french fries might spell convenience for hungry people today, but they take a back burner to the home-style meals she prepared for our family years ago in Piedmont. Mom managed nicely without a self-cleaning oven with temperature and timing controls, or a modern refrigerator with freezer and ice-cube dispenser, not to mention a microwave oven, slow cooker, garbage disposal or dishwasher.

Mom kept perishables such as meat and dairy products in a rather small wooden icebox. A block of ice was placed in the top section, and food was stored in the bottom. A deep pan under the icebox caught the *drip, drip, drip* of melting ice. A mop stood nearby, ready to come to the rescue in case the pan overflowed.

Mom planned meals for eight children, Dad and herself, and everyone gathered to eat around the large kitchen table.

> *On Sundays we usually had beef roast cooked with potatoes, and a vegetable side dish. And we had plenty of homemade bread. Who worried about calories?*

On Sundays we usually had beef roast cooked with potatoes, and a vegetable side dish. And we had plenty of homemade bread. Who worried about calories?

Any leftover beef was cut up the next day and cooked with potatoes and whatever else Mom put into the Monday-night hash.

During the week, Mom usually prepared a boiled dinner—green beans and corn or cabbage and potatoes flavored with two or three chunks of pork salt side. We kids always thought Dad was kidding, but he said he'd rather eat salt side than chicken!

When we had hamburgers, Mom would place a nice slice of onion inside each patty and when the burgers were done, the onion would be tender and tasty. I believe that was in the days before cheeseburgers had been invented!

Of course, Friday was fish night, and I enjoyed the way Mom prepared it. She dipped it in cornmeal and flour and fried it in a skillet. Rounding out the meal was cooked macaroni to which tomatoes and longhorn cheese had been added. Once in a while we had salmon

croquettes covered with tomato ketchup.

Saturday was soup day. Mom put a large, meaty soup bone in a pot half-full of water and brought it to a boil to make flavorful beef stock. After she added all kinds of vegetables, salt, pepper and other seasonings, she let the soup simmer slowly for the rest of the afternoon.

Dad raised chickens in the back yard; occasionally he would catch one or two plump ones, sending them to eternity with a hatchet.

The birds were soaked in hot water, then dressed, cut up, dipped in flour, and cooked to golden brown in a big iron skillet. Mashed potatoes and chicken gravy were also on the menu, plus succotash perhaps, and thick-sliced bread.

Chicken necks, wings and backs were set aside for rice or noodle soup which tasted oh, so good at lunchtime on school days.

During hunting season in autumn, we could purchase rabbits at the local butcher shop. Even after the rabbits were cleaned, cut up and fried, we had to be careful not to bite into buckshot!

My dad, a B & O machinist who worked at the shops in Keyser, would stop at a butcher shop now and then and bring home beef kidneys, liver or tongues to add variety to our evening meals. I can tell you one thing: Kidney stew isn't delectable when cold.

He also bought pudding at the butcher shop. Mom cooked cornmeal and mixed it into the pudding to make ponhaus. After cooling overnight, it was sliced and fried for breakfast the next morning, and we ate it topped with butter, jelly or apple butter.

Ever eat sugar syrup on pancakes or buckwheats? We did when Mom couldn't find regular syrup in the pantry cupboard. Sugar syrup is sugar boiled in water.

Wilted lettuce was our favorite salad. Mom fried slices of bacon, then removed them from the bacon grease and drained them. To the bacon grease in the pan she added vinegar, sugar and water, and heated it all together.

She poured the hot mixture over a large bowl of leaf lettuce and garnished the dish with the crumbled bacon strips, hard-cooked eggs and sliced onion.

Mom baked bread and rolls and cakes, but Dad was in charge of the pie-baking, his specialty being raisin.

Leftover pie crust was rolled thin, cut up, sprinkled with butter, sugar and cinnamon, and popped into the oven. We called these johnnycakes. We made fried scones from leftover bread dough.

Toward summer's end, Mom was busy "putting up" sliced cucumber pickles, relishes, tomatoes, corn, etc., which she stored in the cellar cupboard for use during the coming winter.

In the autumn, neighbors came to our home to make apple butter. They all sat around the kitchen table to peel, core and cut up the apples. Early in the morning, they put the prepared apples into a large copper kettle which rested on a sturdy metal framework over a fire. The neighbors took turns stirring the apples with a large wooden paddle at the end of a long pole. The cooking was completed at about dusk when the apple butter was ladled into crocks and sealed with paraffin.

They also retrieved several pennies which had been placed in the kettle before cooking began to keep the apple butter from scorching in the bottom of the kettle. After a day of cooking in the hot apples, the pennies were bright and shiny.

In those good old days, I learned to make vegetable soup and roll out pie crust by watching Mom and Dad in the kitchen. I'm sure happy I was there—and my wife is, too! ❖

The Old Stockpot

By Elizabeth Cole

Mama made stock on Tuesdays and Saturdays, for those were the days when she had long, continuous fires—Tuesdays for heating the iron, and Saturdays for baking bread. In this way she economized on wood, heat and time.

Mama's range was huge, but she kept it black and shiny with a little stove black and lots of elbow grease.

The range had six holes on top, a big oven with a hot closet underneath and, behind the high shelf, a circulating boiler connected to the hot-water delivery pipe.

Mama saved the bones from roasts and poultry, as well as juices left in the meat platters and the water in which most vegetables had been cooked. All of these went into the stockpot. She cracked bones on her bread board with a meat cleaver, covered them with cold water, and brought the mixture slowly to a boil on the front of the range.

Then she pushed the kettle to the back of the stove and simmered the broth for an hour or so. She let me add an onion in which I had stuck 12 cloves, a bay leaf, a few celery tops and a carrot cut into chunks. She simmered this for another hour or so. Then she took it off the range, let it cool a bit, and strained it through cheesecloth.

She taught me to make tomato soup. To a pint of stock I added a pint of her good canned tomatoes, which I had diced, and simmered them together for about an hour.

Sometimes we had clear soup. I simply heated the stock, seasoned with a little salt.

Other times I added a little leftover rice or macaroni, and we had a good, rich soup. For cream of celery, I covered diced celery with cold stock, added a quart of water, and simmered it for about 2 hours. Then I added a pint of milk—nowadays they call it half-and-half.

Mama taught me that all made-over dishes are more savory when stock is used instead of water. I follow Mama's advice to this day and always have stock on hand. I have to buy soup bones and simmer them on the range, then store the stock in the refrigerator. It's really not much bother when weighed against the compliments I get for my cooking.

My family and friends tell me one of their favorites is my Brown Tomato Sauce served over hamburg steaks. I have been making this for the better part of 80 years, so it is second nature for me. After I remove the steaks from the pan, I add 1 tablespoon flour to the grease and mix it. While the flour is browning I fill my measuring cup half-full with strained diced canned tomatoes, then fill the cup to the top with stock. I pour the mixture into the roux and stir until it boils for a few minutes. I add a dash of salt and pepper, then pour the sauce over the hamburgs.

Today I live on a Social Security check. Food prices are so high; I'm glad that Mama taught me that poverty in no way affects the need for skill in preparing food.

So, when you wonder whatever became of those good meals we had back in the Good Old Days, also ponder this question: Whatever became of the old stockpot? ❖

John Slobodnik

Thanksgiving Without a Bite Of Bread

By Gladys Chambless

When that Thanksgiving Day dawned it was dark and threatening. Although we had some rows of scrapping cotton to pick that morning with Mama, we planned a Thanksgiving dinner—in spite of the fact that we didn't have flour, meal, loaf bread, buns or crackers in the house.

There were eight of us—six children, Mama and our stepfather, whom we called "Pa Belk." We lived on the Mount Joy Road side of Prospect Mountain in the far side of Cullman County in north-central Alabama, and we were sharecroppers.

The five of us school-age children had stayed out of school that Wednesday, trying to finish picking our scrap cotton and get it all out before Thanksgiving Day. Pa Belk hadn't had time to go to the mill to get our corn ground the Saturday before last, and when Brother Dave had taken corn to the mill late on the Saturday evening before Thanksgiving, the mill was broken down. There was no meal that week, and no flour either, because the store down at Old Bremen had run out.

Mama had cooked the last of our meal the Monday before, and the last of our flour that Wednesday at dinnertime.

Mama had cooked the last of our meal the Monday before, and the last of our flour that Wednesday at dinnertime—except for the little dab of meal and flour she had saved, she said, just in case she "needed a little thickenin'." She didn't know what in the world we were going to do without a bite of bread in the house for supper and Thanksgiving dinner the following day.

Pa Belk and we older children knew Mama would manage some way so we would eat good and plentiful that Wednesday night, and for Thanksgiving, too. We knew in our hearts that we would not go lacking, no matter what.

Wednesday evening late, as we were coming in from the field, we learned that every one of our nearest neighbors was in just about the same fix. There were six families, including us. Not only was the mill at Old Bremen broken down, but so were the mills at Beech Grove (a few miles the other side of us) and Arkedelphia Mill (nearly in Walker

County). And the merchants in these places had sold out of flour and loaf bread, as well as meal. Pa never thought to buy any crackers; just wasn't used to falling back on crackers for bread. Few merchants in those days kept buns or loaf bread for country folks' emergencies.

That Wednesday evening Mama had cooked a big old dinner pot of butter beans, baked an ovenful of sweet taters and cooked a pot of collards for vegetables.

She took some of the cooked beans from the pot, mashed them, thickened them with that little dab of flour she had saved "just in case," made them out in patties and fried them nice to take the place of bread at supper that night.

With all that good food to eat, we made out mighty well that night after a hard day's work in the cotton field.

Because we were a family with a very smart and managing mama, we went to bed with full and satisfied stomachs, and the assurance that we'd have a good, big Thanksgiving dinner the next day.

Mama was pretty—a tallish-like woman of 42, with dark, graying hair and a fair complexion. She was one of the best managers in a tight fix I ever knew.

Pa Belk was a graying man of 48. He was stepdaddy to me, sister Jo, and brothers Dave, Henry and Maurice. Mama and Pa Belk's baby was our baby brother Elmo, 2 years old.

What a happy family we were! Certainly we had seen hard times, but never before had we gotten into a fix where we had not a bite of bread in the house. But no one was to blame; Mama declared that it was simply "the way of Providence"—whatever that meant—and that was how we all took it.

The next morning, Sis and I were up bright and early to help Mama cook breakfast. What do you think we cooked? A pan of homemade grits—and we made patties out of what was left of the butter beans, and cooked a skillet of cornmeal gravy out of the "little dab" of cornmeal. With molasses, butter, the grits, butter

bean patties, cornmeal gravy and coffee for Mom and Pa Belk, we couldn't have asked for a more satisfying breakfast.

Afterward there was work to do. We left Mama to milk the cows, wash the dishes and make the beds. At 7, Maurice was old enough to help Mama and tend to little Elmo. Pa Belk took care of the barn work and feeding, and set about getting up some firewood, as it certainly was getting colder.

We four older children—Sis, who was just past 16; Dave, 14; Henry, 10; and I, 18—grabbed our pick sacks and slowly wended our way out to the cotton patch, chattering all the way. (Sis and I were old enough to get married if we wanted to, but talking between ourselves, we had declared we never wanted to marry and leave each other and Mama and Pa Belk.)

We were just finishing our cotton scrapping at about 9:30 a.m. when a soft, wavy drizzle swished over our little patch of the world. It wasn't enough to really wet us, but it dampened the cotton. With a snatch, a pull and a promise we plucked the last bolls.

Then, hollering as we always did when we finished field work for the season, we yelled, "Folks in the field picking cotton, cotton in the field and the bolls all rotten!"

We hurried to the barn and threw our sacks onto the loaded wagon under the side shed. What we'd picked that morning just finished a bale—the 15th we'd made and picked that year, but only half of the crop was ours.

By now cold rain was pelting down, so we rushed into the house to catch our breath by the fireplace and dry off a bit. Then we hurried into the kitchen to see what was cooking and help get our Thanksgiving dinner ready. Our big old striking clock on the mantel showed six minutes to 10 a.m.

Mama had a big pot of black-eyed peas boiling over an open eye on the back of the big old range. In her 2-gallon aluminum stewer, one of her big, young Rhode Island Red roosters cooked away, nearly ready for the rice to be added. In the oven she was baking a big pan of Irish taters to take the place of bread.

Maurice had parched a pan of peanuts and was shelling them to add to the peas for seasoning. (We were nearly out of lard, too; planned to kill hogs tomorrow if it were cold enough. And it looked like it might be.)

Quickly I peeled three big sweet taters and cut them up to boil for sweet tater pudding while Sis churned the milk. Dave and Henry peel and cored about two dozen ripe fall apples from our own rented trees. I filled the core of each with sugar and placed them in the big roasting pan for baking.

I spiced the pudding with cinnamon and sprinkled brown maple sugar on top. A few minutes before Mama added seasoned rice to the chicken, Sis finished the churning and had a big bowl of butter.

Then, hollering as we always did when we finished field work for the season, we yelled, "Folks in the field picking cotton, cotton in the field and the bolls all rotten!"

She helped me cut up a few rashers of white meat and add it, along with some sliced Irish potatoes and onions, to the pot of sauerkraut Mama was heating on the back of the stove.

Henry and Dave had measured out a gallon of seed beer and put it outside to cool for our special dinner.

And so, with stewed chicken and rice, boiled peas and peanuts, leftover collards, the kraut dish, sweet tater pud-ding and baked apples for dessert, Irish taters for bread and seed beer to drink, we really fared well, and enjoyed one of the most thankful Thanksgiving dinners ever.

Pa Belk even asked a very special blessing for, as he said, we could have been without any other food on that day besides bread.

But we were now also out of lard, and it continued to rain until late Saturday evening so there was no hog killing. We had no meal or flour till bedtime Saturday night, when Pa Belk and Dave returned from Old Bremen.

There had been many turns of corn ahead of them, and of course they had had to wait their turn. While they were waiting, Pa Belk had thought to buy a sack of flour.

We were not the only family in such a fix. As I said, we made out even if much of our food was gassy food. I and other members of our family who are still alive have not forgotten that Thanksgiving in 1926 when we hadn't a bite of bread in the house. ❖

The Turkey That Saved Our Lives

By Esther Norman

November 1936—St. Joseph, Mo. Following the most terrible Depression in U.S., times were slowly getting better. But my husband was still laid off, and we faced a bleak Thanksgiving.

One day I tuned in radio station KMA in Shenandoah, Iowa. The station's owner, Earl May, was famous in Iowa, Missouri and the other Midwestern states not only for his seed and nursery operation, but for his dandy radio station. Its homey programming appealed to average, everyday families like ours. It was one of my favorite stations.

I was feeling as blue as I thought it was possible to feel because I thought we wouldn't have a Thanksgiving Day worth remembering. Then I tuned in to KMA as I dried the breakfast dishes. KMA played a swingy tune, *Three Little Fishies*, and then *Flat-Footed Floogee*. Then I heard the announcer say, "Here's a dandy contest for all you listeners to enter. Look at the prizes! Thanksgiving turkeys!"

> *I stopped, entranced. Oh, boy! What I wouldn't give to win a Thanksgiving turkey and surprise my husband for the holiday!*

I stopped, entranced. Oh, boy! What I wouldn't give to win a Thanksgiving turkey and surprise my husband for the holiday!

The announcer continued: "Just write a simple letter telling why you like KMA radio station. Send it to Shenandoah, Iowa. If you are lucky, you'll receive a big, 16-pound turkey in time for Thanksgiving."

A simple letter, I thought. Could I write a simple letter that would win a turkey? I decided I would try to think of the reasons why I liked the station.

It was a friendly station, and Earl May often spoke his mind about subjects which interested all of us. And he often laughed at himself.

I jotted down all the ideas I could think of while listening to KMA. I tried to think up even more, but my thoughts would roam. …

~

I wanted to go see Shirley Temple in one of her wonderful movies like *Little Miss Marker* or *The Littlest Rebel* or *Captain January*. I had seen her very first movie, which was—I believe—*Stand Up and Cheer* in about 1934. I thought she was the dearest, sweetest little girl I had ever seen. How she could dance and sing! How she could smile! I read that her salary was $300,000 a year, and I just couldn't believe there was that much money in the world!

~

I sighed. Here I was, a young married woman, trying to write a letter that might win a turkey so our Thanksgiving table would hold something good to eat. We didn't have much in the pantry. I laughed, thinking what a sight it would be if we had only potatoes and onions for our main dish on that special day. My thoughts strayed again. …

~

The news was on, and President Franklin D. Roosevelt was mentioned often. There was also news of all the gang-sters, and all the killings and stealing that had been going on. I thought about how many had been killed after infamous careers—like John Dillinger, Baby Face Nelson, Pretty Boy Floyd and Machine Gun Kelly. The latter was the one who had yelled, "Don't shoot, G-men!" He meant "government men," and the name stuck.

~

To stop my daydreaming, I turned off the little radio. I could concentrate better in the silence. I thought about what I would miss if I didn't have my wonderful radio. My, what it meant to me! Then I wrote my letter.

I told how the operators and personnel seemed like "home folks" and "friends," how they seemed to have a friendly interest in my family and all of us ordinary people in the Midwest. I told how they made my life more pleasant and kept me in tune with the times. I said I got a lot of help from the household hints and recipes so dear to women's hearts, and I enjoyed getting "the scoop" while I did my housework, without having to read a newspaper. They sold coffee and other products besides seeds, and I told them how much I enjoyed their products and appreciated their low prices.

A few days before Thanksgiving, I was thrilled to hear Earl May read my letter on the radio! I was so excited I could hardly stand the suspense. He said it was "in the running," as was every letter read on the air. My husband said not to get my hopes up, however, as there was no fast way to get a turkey from Shenandoah, Iowa, to someone in St. Joseph, Mo.

I sort of gave up. I figured a turkey would spoil, coming all that distance—it was about 125 miles, after all. Cars didn't go too fast in those days. As I grew convinced they couldn't send me a turkey quickly, I felt sadder than ever.

A couple of days later we were sitting at the table, having a cup of hot tea and trying to act as if we had plenty of money. There was a loud knock at the door— and there stood a deliveryman holding a big package. We thanked him, then carried the box to the kitchen. When we opened it we found a huge turkey from KMA!

"It weighs 16 pounds!" I gasped. "It's the most beautiful turkey I ever saw in my life!"

My husband hugged me. "Thanks to you, we're going to have a wonderful Thanksgiving, after all!"

"Boydie will get some good dinners, too," I said happily. Boydie, our dog, hadn't had a meal of meat for ages, but he loved us anyway.

So on Thanksgiving in 1936, we baked the big turkey with plenty of sage dressing. It turned out so beautifully that we took some snapshots with our cheap little Brownie camera. In one (above), I held the platter with the 16-pound turkey on it.

What a day! We were the happiest young married couple in the world. The next evening we had some friends in for big, hefty sandwiches of white turkey meat with sweet pickles and hot coffee. They praised it to the skies. It really was the finest, most wonderful turkey I ever tasted. ❖

Old-Time Recipes

Vinegar

My elderly aunt said she found this vinegar recipe in a notebook of handwritten recipes that were used when she was a girl at home. She gave me a copy of it. She was born in 1900, so this recipe was used in the 1800s.

1 gallon clover blossoms
10 pounds sugar
1 cup dried yeast
1 gallon rainwater

Mix all ingredients in a large jar. Cover with cloth and let stand for 4 weeks. After the 4th week, strain the liquid and put it in jugs. It will be ready for use within a short time.

—*Flo Burtnett*

Mint Jelly

2 pounds apples
½ cup mint leaves *or*
  ½ teaspoon mint extract
3 cups sugar
Green vegetable coloring

Wash and quarter apples; barely cover with boiling water and cook, covered, until very soft. Strain through cloth. Measure 1 quart juice and add crushed mint leaves. Cook slowly 20 minutes; strain. Reheat to boiling; add sugar; cook until syrup sheets off spoon. Add coloring. Seal in hot, sterilized glasses. Makes 6 (6-ounce) glasses.

Grandma Catherine Whistler's Hickory Nut Cake

1½ cups sugar
4 egg whites
½ cup butter
¾ cup milk
2 cups flour
2 teaspoons baking powder
1 cup hickory nuts *or* walnuts

Because of all the nuts, this is a very filling cake. While the recipe is just as good as it was originally written more than 100 years ago, we find we like it better if we add 1 additional teaspoon baking powder, 1 teaspoon salt and 1 teaspoon vanilla extract to the batter.

After baking, it can be iced with vanilla buttercream frosting to which ¼ teaspoon maple flavoring has been added.

—*E.L. Moore*

Looking Back Some 60 Years

By Nelle Portrey Davis

All around us today, changes in lifestyles are rampant. Economic pressures are to blame in some instances; disillusionment with contemporary living is responsible in others. Whatever the cause, increasing numbers of people both young and old are hankering for the "good old days."

As a result, thrift, frugality and conservation are again being recognized as desirable traits, even by many modern people. Higher prices, hurried living and the tension encouraged by modern life are causing an interest in the ways of a bygone era.

Homegrown foods are again in favor. Many city dwellers who can't raise their own food are eager to find markets where homegrown organic foods can be purchased. They want to serve good meals without resorting to processed or prepared foods.

In the good old days, bakery bread was unknown. I know of no homier smell than that of baking bread. Baking is not difficult and does not require a great deal of strength, time or skill. No preservatives or chemicals were added to our baking, and so it was more healthful than the modern bakery bread (especially if whole-wheat flour was used) and the cost was far less. An extra bonus was the pan of cinnamon rolls or coffee cake which was usually made from the last of the dough.

Some housewives used a yeast starter, renewed or refreshed with each baking, but we made, dried and stored our own dry yeast.

But now comes the truly old-fashioned part of bread-making: The yeast was homemade. Some housewives used a yeast starter, renewed or refreshed with each baking, but we made, dried and stored our own dry yeast, and many women preferred this to the starter method. Made from boiled hops, cornmeal and water into which the yeast starter was incorporated, the mass was rolled into small balls, flattened, dried thoroughly and stored in a covered container in a cool, dry place.

The process of making bread with this yeast required more time, as the yeast was added to warm water and "the sponge" set in the evening.

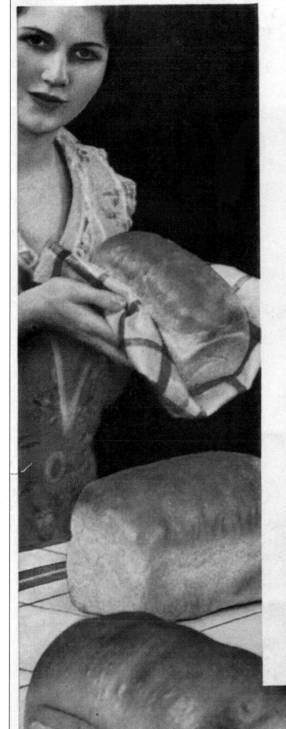

HAVE YOU TRIED *the modern concentrated form of easy-to-eat yeast—YEAST FOAM TABLETS?* *Let us send you a free "get-acquainted" sample of these delicious health tablets of pure pasteurized yeast.*

Reduce your Food Bill

....by eating this delicious, healthful, *home-made* bread

Eat more bread ... bread baked in your own oven with Yeast Foam or Magic Yeast. It's one of the most wholesome and healthful foods you can consume—and one of the least expensive. Home-made bread, baked with either of these famous yeasts, has a rich creamy flavor all its own—a delicious tastiness that gratifies everyone's longing for real home-made bread. There is nothing like it. Try Yeast Foam or Magic Yeast for bread, coffee cake, rolls or griddle cakes. Our illustrated booklet, "The Art of Making Bread," tells exactly what to do to insure success. And it's all so easy and simple that you'll be delighted. The booklet is free and we'll take pleasure in sending it postpaid on your request.

ON THE AIR EVERY SUNDAY *from 3:30 to 4:00 P. M., Eastern Standard Time, the melodious* "YEAST FOAMERS" *over N. B. C.— WJZ and all supplementary stations from coast to coast.*

Just the same except in name

Package of five cakes at your grocer's 10c

NORTHWESTERN YEAST COMPANY
1744 N. Ashland Avenue, Chicago, Illinois

Please send me descriptive booklets on ☐ yeast for better bread; ☐ yeast for health; ☐ yeast for poultry.

Name...

Address................................... City..........

Old-Time advertisement reprinted from the December 1933 issue of The Farmer's Wife.

In a warm place, the yeast worked and expanded overnight. The dough was mixed and kneaded the next morning. If a warm place for the rising was not available, the stone jar or crock containing the sponge was wrapped in a heavy blanket or old quilt to keep the yeast from chilling.

Of course, homes in rural districts did not have electricity. We lived in prairie country, which had no trees for firewood. Using coal meant both an outlay of cash and a long drive with team and wagon to haul it. We used what was needed, but you can be sure that it was not wasted. In emergencies we gathered cow chips on the prairie. They burned well, but gave less heat than wood or coal. Plus, they did not last as long and made lots of ashes. But they sometimes saved a trip to town during a busy time.

Corncobs made a satisfactory fire, though they burned out quickly. We always had hogs fattening on corn, and it was unthinkable that the cobs should not be used in some way. To encourage the morning fire in an icy kitchen stove or the "front room" heater, there was always a tin can of kerosene behind the kitchen stove, with three or four corncobs immersed in the oil—a certain way to get the fire off to an early, quick start.

It was about 1906 when Mother built a gadget that not only conserved fuel but made it unnecessary to keep the kitchen hot during the summer to serve a hot meal. Her contrivance was a "fireless cooker." Commercial models had lately come on the market and were considered quite the thing by the smart housewives who could afford them. Mother made her own.

She built a wooden box about 3 feet long, 18 inches wide and 24 inches tall. She nailed together a flat lid for the top. Then the box was filled with prairie hay, packed in as tightly as possible, but leaving a hollow nest at each end—one large enough to hold her gallon-size

gray granite kettle, and the other the correct size to accommodate her smallest iron pot.

In the morning while the kitchen range was fired, she would start her dinner—probably a pot roast, well browned in the cast-iron skillet. Then it went into the preheated little iron pot where it was surrounded by potatoes and whatever other vegetables were to be served—turnips, carrots or onions.

A little water was added, the whole was sprinkled with salt and pepper, and with the pot thoroughly heated on the stove and tightly covered, it was settled down into its nest of hay in the "fireless cooker." That was for dinner, the main midday meal. The other pot might contain boiling-hot beans and a chunk of salt pork or a ham bone for the evening supper.

With the lids firmly in place, a heavy old blanket was tucked snugly over the kettles and the lid was put on the chest. At mealtime the food was done to a turn. No turning or stirring was needed and there was no danger of food sticking or burning.

As a finishing touch, Mother padded the top of her cooker with an old quilt and upholstered it with a patchwork cover. It made a very nice seat in the kitchen.

So many of our modern supermarket purchases are things we did not dream of buying 60 years ago. Salad dressings and mayonnaise did not come in bottles at the store. They were made at home, and the ingredients were wholesome foods, not additives with unpronounceable names and unknown origins. Every housewife knew how to make a variety of salad dressings simply and inexpensively.

Jams and jellies! They were a delight to make, lovely to look at, an object of pride when set on the shelves, and delicious to eat! To conserve fuel and keep the house cooler in summer, fruit pulps and juices were usually canned during the fruit season, then made into jams and jellies in the winter when the heat from the range was welcome.

And the soup kettle! I never hear of one nowadays. "The French are the best cooks in the world," Mother was wont to say, "and they always have a soup kettle simmering on the back of the stove." So did Mother, during the winter months.

Today we can store leftovers in the electric refrigerator. But in Mother's kitchen, her soup kettle served as a storage place for leftover vegetables, meat scraps and bits of gravy. Bones from the roast, leftover dabs of green beans, corn, carrots, onions and peas all went into the pot. Seasonings were added as needed along with rice, barley, cubed potatoes or egg rivels, and every winter evening there was a pot of hearty soup to start our meal. If she lacked a soup bone for stock, Mother boiled the vegetables and then added a quart of whole milk a few minutes before serving. Today I find that a lump of oleo and dry milk work quite as well.

Our noodles were homemade. I don't think we knew there was any other kind—and possibly there was not 60 years ago. Anyway, who, after eating old-fashioned homemade noodles, would ever be satisfied with any other kind? We made quantities of paper-thin noodles when eggs were plentiful and low in price, and stored them for future use.

Today we are constantly warned against using animal fat for food. Making soap seems to be a lost art, yet it is very simple, involving little time and almost no expense. And it is such a practical way to utilize any kind of animal fat.

I have mentioned the lack of refrigeration. We did have food-cooling methods of a sort. Mother had a homemade structure in which she could keep milk and butter cool. It hung on the north side of the house. It was about 3 feet tall and 18 inches square. The top and bottom were solid; there were 2-inch slats at the corners and the sides were left open and hung with gunny-sacks that had been ripped open and washed.

On top of this cooler was a dishpan of water. The burlap curtain extended at the top so it was immersed in the water. Hence, by capillarity, the water seeped down the sides of the box and kept the interior cool enough so that butter stayed firm and milk stayed sweet.

We also used the cellar to keep food from spoiling. It was always cool and pleasant there, even in the hottest weather. Neighbors with open wells hung their milk and butter in the well to keep it cool and sweet.

Our prairie country knew no running springs, but during our sojourn in the Ozarks we found many springhouses—snug little houses built over a spring, with the water run-ning through. They had natural rock floors, and there cans and jugs of cold milk were kept im-mersed in the running water. Watermelons were also brought in the early morning and left there to cool.

Lacking a springhouse, others often built a huge box with a hinged lid over a spring. One frequently saw these on rented farms, where the tenant did not care to build a springhouse on another man's place.

In those days, it was not so much a case of conserving energy or fuel as it was of simply having the needed fuel or energy available. ❖

Grandma's Pearl Tea

By Marilyn Baker

Of all the stories Mother told me about growing up during the Depression, none so moves me as the story of Granny Walker's Pearl Tea.

⁓

Mother grew up on a farm in Missouri in the 1920s and 1930s. They were years of doing without.

In the winter, the children each had one pair of shoes. In the summer they went barefoot. The girls had two dresses—one for church and one for school. Both were usually homemade from feed sacks.

Toys were scarce. My mother and her sister played with dolls made from old socks. My uncle's toy "airplanes" were corncobs with a chicken feather stuck in the end.

Still, my mother has fond memories of those times. She remembers fishing in the creek, receiving her first doll with a real china head, and a rare licorice stick or "jawbreaker" from town. Best of all, Mother recalls the weekly trip to Granny Walker's for Pearl Tea.

Every Sunday afternoon my grandfather would hitch up the buggy for the 9-mile trek to my Great-Grandmother Walker's house. Granny Walker lived alone in a big, white, two-story house on a hill. My mother thought it was the finest house she had ever seen.

From her stories, I can almost see the wide porch with its creaking porch swing. Inside, the gracefully curved bannisters led upstairs to huge bedrooms with brass feather beds and rose-covered rugs on the polished wood floors. Farther up, the attic was stacked with boxes and trunks filled with big flowered hats, satin ballgowns and Grandpa Walker's Confederate uniform.

But my mother's favorite room was the parlor downstairs.

She tells of tables laden with bric-a-brac that small hands were careful not to touch. Facing each other were two big sofas on which a small girl could curl up to hide her dirty bare feet.

An old piano stood in one corner. Sometimes the children could coax Granny to play Two Little Orphans so they could cry and cry and have a wonderful time. It was in this parlor that Granny served her Pearl Tea.

When hands were washed and everyone was seated, Granny would emerge from the kitchen bearing a silver tray. Each person would receive a delicate china cup filled with hot, sweet liquid. Mother would balance her cup and saucer on her lap so as not to spill a single precious drop. Sitting in the midst of her family, feeling warm, loved and very grown-up, Mother would sip this special drink that only Granny knew how to make. Nothing before or since, she says, has ever tasted so good.

"Mama, how come we never have Pearl Tea here at home?"

One day when she was older, Mother asked her mother, "Mama, how come we never have Pearl Tea here at home? Is it because Granny is so rich?"

"Granny isn't rich, Honey. She lost all her money when the banks closed."

She sat my mother down on the kitchen chair. "There's something I'm going to tell you. But you must never let on to Granny. She's very proud. Pearl Tea is special. It's special because it's served with grace and shared with those she loves. But it really isn't tea."

"What is it?" Mother asked, wide-eyed and eager to learn the secret of Pearl Tea at last.

"It's just hot water, dear. Hot water with milk and sugar."

⁓

I never knew Granny Walker. She died long before I was born. I didn't grow up in a depression, nor did I ever know what it was like to be really poor. But I sometimes wonder if we all wouldn't be better off with a little less champagne and a lot more Pearl Tea in our lives. ❖

Flour by the Ton

By Naomi Bishop
As told by her husband

My mother always complained that her pantry was too small, although it was as large as many modern kitchens. There was a narrow aisle down its center, bordered on one side by a wide "molding board" table. Opposite were two large storage bins for flour and sugar. Several 7-gallon lard cans, filled to the brim just after hog butchering, stood beside the bins. Shelves climbing the walls were loaded with staples—molasses, salt, Postum, vinegar.

Since we lived 12 wagon miles from town and there were 14 of us counting Dad and Ma, my father bought staples in quantity. Flour came a ton at a time—40 50-pound sacks of it. The bin in the pantry held 100 pounds. The rest went to the attic, where we stacked the sacks crisscrossed atop one another. We surrounded the resulting white mountain with mousetraps. It was my special chore to empty and rebait them. I was unusually diligent, as each victim meant a nickel in my pocket.

I can still see Ma kneading great batches of bread at the molding board, which was always scrubbed as white as pine could be. I wish I had a nickel for every loaf of bread she carried from that pantry to the old round oak oven.

The pans held three loaves each, and the oven held four pans. Ma baked twice a week. Once the oven was hot, she did her other baking—pies, cakes and cookies by the dozen. They cooled on the lower shelves in an array which tantalized the eyes no less than the nose.

On baking day we hurried home from school faster than usual. The aroma greeted us at the end of the lane. We knew the treat that awaited us. Ma did the inexcusable, according to most bread-making instructions: She let us slice the heels off the bread while the loaves were still hot. Once I'd spread that heel with sweet butter, I would not have traded it for a piece of pie or cake. I *might* have traded it for a cookie filled with mincemeat; those were my favorite—and literally my downfall.

In our family of 11 boys and only one baby girl, one boy was assigned to help with the household chores. Because I was small and unsuited for heavy outdoor work, I usually had the job. I must have been a great help, too, for I followed Ma's instructions to the letter.

For instance, when she told me to measure out 7 cups of syrup for mincemeat cookies, I took seven cups from their hooks, filled each with syrup, and then asked, "There, that's done. What comes next?"

One Saturday I helped Ma all morning with the cleaning. That afternoon she and Dad took the younger children to call on a neighbor. The older boys were pitching horseshoes at the corral. I was alone in the house—alone with those mincemeat cookies! I climbed onto a lard can to reach the shelf where the cookie can stood.

When Ma came home a few minutes later, her first question was, "Why on earth didn't you use the footstool?" I couldn't answer. Tears were streaming from my face, joining the lard which dripped down from my waist and puddled in greasy white masses at my feet. I didn't know why I hadn't used the footstool; all I knew was the deep resentment I felt toward that darned lard-can lid which had collapsed, dumping me into the lard.

Resentment was of no use, however, nor were tears. My punishment was hours spent removing every vestige of the mess I had made. That particular memory still makes me a bit sick to my stomach. But Ma's pantry was the greatest room in the house! ❖

We Never Ate a Toadstool

By Frances Russell

My cousin and I were eavesdropping on the women in the kitchen as they tried to decide what to do with a soggy gray fruitcake. A new bride had proudly brought it to the Christmas feast—but she had baked it using canned fruit with the juice instead of candied fruit.

"We'll give it to the young'uns with the cast-iron stomachs." They meant us! "If they don't eat it we'll just have to throw it out." We ate it.

They probably weren't surprised, considering that they knew we had eaten worse things. There was the time we ate most of a box of chocolates my aunt's boyfriend had brought. While they spooned in the parlor with eyes only for each other, we snitched the candy and ate it under the bedclothes in the dark bedroom. It didn't bother us—much— to discover next morning that the few pieces remaining in the box were filled with little white worms.

Growing up in the Appalachian Mountains during the Depression, we ate, drank, smoked and chewed anything.

Growing up in the Appalachian Mountains during the Depression, we ate, drank, smoked and chewed everything and anything—not because of any nutritional deficiency, because even during those lean years we had good, plain, nourishing food which came from the land on which we lived. But compared to our gastronomical experiences and experiments, table food and "good-for-you" food was uninteresting. Besides, unless we cooked it ourselves, we liked our food raw.

Perched in the highest branches with a salt shaker, we ate tiny green apples. Our vegetable garden had a hard time growing crops to maturity, for we pulled just-emerged rhubarb, radishes and onions. We ate tomatoes and cucumbers as soon as they were recognizable. We ate barely kerneled corn, raw potatoes, watermelon rind, sour grass, grass grass, mayapples, green gooseberries (the sourest of all the sour things we ever ate), rose petals and clover blossoms. We pulled morning glory and honeysuckle blooms and sucked the sweet nectar from their stems.

In winter we made snow ice cream, sometimes with not-so-clean snow, and milk, sugar and vanilla. We ate icicles, which tasted slightly like the tarred roof from which they hung. We made fudge and taffy that was always grainy; it never hardened, so we ate it with a spoon.

In the fall we swung in tall trees, Tarzan-style, to pick wild grapes from the vines entwined in the branches. We fermented them in big crocks with sugar we had swapped for eggs at the country store. We were always fermenting something in all seasons—dandelions, blackberries, raisins when we could get them, and a wine made from honey which we thought must be blessed by angels while we slept.

For a time, we made home brew in the smokehouse loft. But we were forced to give that up after a big batch, probably with too much yeast or too tightly corked, exploded one night and leaked through the cracks in the loft floor, dripping slivers of glass and foam onto the cured Virginia hams below.

After that, we depended on samples of white lightnin' from stills hidden in the backwoods. We never told their locations for fear of our lives, for bootleggers were secretive and trusted us only because they knew we were as scared of getting caught as they were. (They were scared of the sheriff; we were scared of our grandmother.) But we could judge a "runoff" of moonshine with the best of them, and talked knowingly of the "bead" and taste. Actually, we seldom did more than taste it, for the vile-smelling stuff was too much, even for us.

We chewed tobacco and got deathly sick. To make matters worse, we were dosed with castor oil, and when we survived that, with molasses and sulphur. In our weakened state we were convinced we were being poisoned. We gave up tobacco, but smoked cigars made of grapevine, and became experts at rolling cigarettes with tissue paper and something (I still wonder what) called "life everlasting."

Sometimes we caught crawdads in the creek and cooked them on a little iron stove, boiling them in a rusty tin can.

We fried potatoes, sprinkling them equally with ashes and pepper. Our grandmother sometimes gave us dough, and we made biscuits, kneading them into strange shapes, our hands getting whiter as the dough became grayer.

When we ran out of things to eat, we chewed whatever was handy—celluloid doll arms, rubber baby pants (we sucked bubbles in these and popped them), pencils, coffee grounds, sugar cane stalks. We munched a mixture of cocoa and sugar. We licked Vicks salve.

At hog-killing time, we blew the hogs' bladders into balloons, proving once and for all that we weren't too fastidious about what we put into our mouths.

We went to molasses stir-offs and ate gobs of the sticky hot foam. We made tea from sassafras and ginseng roots. We knew where the best berries grew. We ran barefoot over frosty ground in the early dawn to pick up chestnuts—real chestnuts, which, before we were 10, had blighted and died. We picked chinquapins, getting the burrs in our fingers, hair and clothes. We pounded hulls from bushels of black walnuts, staining our mouths and hands as we ate the unseasoned nutmeats. We found the tenderest mountain tea and ate its leaves and berries.

Some things we ate on a dare—peach seeds (we'd heard they contained arsenic), small seeds of all kinds to see if we'd get appendicitis, and rhubarb leaves. But we never ate a buckeye, and we never ate a toadstool. Somewhere, at some time, someone had warned us so thoroughly about them that, for once, even we were intimidated.

Of course, everybody knew that only half of the buckeye and only half of the toadstool was poisonous, and if you ate the good half, you'd be as wise as Solomon. On the other hand, if you ate the bad half, you could go into violent convulsions and die a horrible death. We spent hours speculating about it, and we always carried a buckeye in our pockets just in case we hit upon which half to eat.

To this day I can't recall why we didn't get up the nerve to try one or the other. Maybe we never put it to a real dare; maybe we waited too long and our curiosity dwindled as we grew toward adolescence. Whatever the reason, I'm sorry that one of us didn't make the supreme sacrifice. Win or lose, we could have been remembered with awe. ❖

"Monkey Stove" Hamburgers

By Virginia Armentaro

We're out of gas!" wailed my sister. A surge of excitement swept through me. Out of gas! I knew what that meant: We could go down to the basement and cook our meals on the monkey stove.

I was 8 and it was the Depression. We lived outside the city limits and bottled gas was the only fuel we had for cooking. When the gas ran out, all we had to do was call the bottle gas company and they would deliver a new bottle the next day. The only catch was that we had to pay on delivery. And since Papa was working only three days a week, the money was hard to come by. Until we had saved enough, my sister had to cook downstairs.

My oldest sister, Marguerite, had reason to lament. My mother had passed away three years earlier. At 13, Marguerite had assumed the responsibility of helping Papa take care of his family of five girls.

We tried to help in our own way, but I think we younger ones just got in the way. Elizabeth was next oldest. Frances was in the middle. I came next; Helen Marie was the littlest.

On this day we girls rushed around Marguerite, volunteering to take various culinary articles downstairs for her. Since Papa was home, he went downstairs to light the stove. Had he not been home, my two oldest sisters would have lit the stove with great care, warning us to stand back.

> *We also had an iron poker with a coiled handle. I loved to watch Papa or my sisters lift a lid so we could peek in at the blazing fire.*

In about half an hour the stove was crackling merrily. Marguerite had been mixing and forming hamburger patties. She brought the skillet downstairs and placed it on the flat surface of the stove.

The monkey stove had four lids and an I-shaped piece of iron with which to hold and lift them. Each lid had an indentation where the handle was inserted. We could open each lid individually to see how the fire was doing.

We also had an iron poker with a coiled handle. I loved to watch Papa or my sisters lift a lid so that we could peek in at the blazing fire.

It seemed almost forever, but finally the tantalizing aroma of hamburgers drifted about the room and floated upstairs to the kitchen where Helen Marie and I were setting the table. We finished quickly and nearly tumbled down the stairs in our haste to get a good look at—and maybe a tiny taste of—the monkey stove fried hamburgers.

Marguerite carefully lifted the hamburgers from the pan. They were much smaller than any you would get at McDonald's or Wendy's because we had to stretch that pound of hamburger as far as it would go.

Elizabeth opened and heated a can of pork and beans. Frances helped her bring the steaming pan upstairs and they poured the contents into a bowl. Papa had made tomato-pepper salad.

At last we were ready to eat!

As I recall, I wasn't too fond of hamburgers in those days. But when they were cooked on that stove, they were delicious! We always had plenty of bread, and that helped fill any empty corners in our stomachs until the next meal.

After supper we did the dishes. We always took turns—but not always willingly. Many times, to make the unpleasant task go faster, we would sing together or play "My Daddy Owns a Grocery Store." The person who was "it" said a letter and the rest of us had to guess which product was in the store.

That evening we did both—the singing and the game—because it took longer to clean the pans, which had become blackened on the monkey stove. I began to understand why Marguerite was not so crazy about cooking downstairs.

Papa had put a fairly large piece of coal in the stove so that it wouldn't go out, because he knew what we'd do next. Instead of putting the skillet away, Marguerite put it aside. We giggled because we knew why.

After the last dish had been put in its proper place, she said, "Shall we go back downstairs?"

"Yes!" we all chorused.

Elizabeth ran to the cupboard and got a big bag of yellow popcorn. Marguerite got the cooking oil and some bowls and we all trooped downstairs again.

She sprinkled popcorn into the skillet. We girls got chairs, a box and Papa's workbench and sat down to wait. Papa had rekindled the fire and turned the damper on the long stove-pipe to regulate the flame as much as possible.

Our basement was not carpeted or paneled as many are today. But we gathered around that little monkey stove in a contented circle. Family

happiness does not necessarily come from surroundings, but from within.

As the popcorn's scent assailed our noses, we giggled and talked. As the kernels popped louder and faster we laughed more. Soon the popping began to slow. Pop … pop … stop.

Marguerite took the skillet off the stove and divided the popcorn among six bowls (Papa had joined us, too). Taking our bowls eagerly, we began to eat. Surely, we thought, our cups runneth over!

We munched the popcorn hungrily. We hoped Papa would have enough money in the next week or two to get the gas. But tonight we were a happy family—full, content and together. Let the gas run out! This was fun! I would never forget it. ❖

Corn Bread And Beans

By J.B. Cearly

Remember the song *Corn Bread and Beans*? It's a lively tune which I have tried to sing many times. Some folks think the song is amusing; others say it is poking fun at poor people during the Depression. Some insist that the lyrics mimic the people of the Old South.

But I feel that it is merely an interesting and truthful tale of the hard times many people experienced. "Got me a job choppin' down cedar trees; Now I'll be eatin' corn bread and beans."

I also think that a good pot of pinto beans and a pan of corn bread is just about the best food you can find anywhere.

The drought and Dust Bowl days in our area of West Texas—often referred to as "the South Plains"—began with severity in 1930 and lasted until 1937. Many farmers and ranchers went broke and had to leave the area. Prices for crops and cattle were extremely low, and the drought compounded the problem.

How did people survive when it didn't rain enough to produce half a crop? The people had the will to endure, and they raised most of their own food.

Our windmill pumped water that was fit for the stock. But it was too salty for human consumption, so unfortunately we couldn't use it to irrigate a garden. We had a cistern for drinking water, but we often had to haul water for home use from a neighbor's place where the water was good.

Dad always plowed our land late in the winter. Then, when it was warm enough in the early spring, we would plant a large patch of pinto beans and other vegetables. He usually planted them after a rain shower. In 1931 we didn't get enough rain for early planting. But one day we got a light shower, so we poured some warm water into a bucket, and filled the bucket with dry pinto beans to soak overnight.

By the next morning, the beans had swollen. We carried that bucket

> *All those meals of corn bread and beans helped us make it through the bleak 1930s. We didn't have money, but we had faith and a purpose to survive.*

of soaked beans to the field and planted them by hand. (People call this "backbreaking work," but it wasn't so bad.) In just a few days those beans began breaking the ground, sending up tender little stems with two leaves. We were very happy about that!

After three days, Dad had his three boys hoe out all the weeds from the patch, and rake dirt around the young bean stems to keep them from drying out and dying. Many people who didn't plow up dirt around their newly sprouted plants lost their crops that year.

Although it was an extremely dry year, the beans produced a fair crop. Mother canned some of the fresh green beans in Mason and Kerr jars. The boys gathered the beans and helped snap them for canning.

When the remaining beans were dry on the stalks, we gathered them by hand and put them in baskets or cotton sacks. Then it was my job to shell the dry beans. I put the bean pods in a cotton sack and, using a 1- by 4-inch board, gently "spanked" the sack from one end to the other. Then I turned the sack over and repeated the process.

After I felt that the beans were separated from the hulls, I poured the sack's contents into a tub. We dipped the beans in a bucket and held it up and let the beans slowly drift down into another tub. The breeze blew the hulls away, leaving only the clean beans behind.

While many of our neighbors had to leave their homes in search of food, we managed to survive on corn bread and beans.

Mother was a hard worker and a good cook. If we didn't have any home-cured meat, she'd buy a ham bone in town. Early in the morning, she'd set a large pot of water to boil. Then she'd add about a pound of dried pinto beans and the ham bone and a little salt and pepper. She kept the beans cooking over a low fire, so that they barely boiled. She checked the pot frequently and added water as needed.

About an hour before lunchtime—when the beans were nearly done—Mother would make a batch of corn muffins or two pie pans of corn bread, using the cornmeal ground from corn we had grown ourselves. She had her own recipe for corn bread which went something like this:

Mother's Corn Bread

1	large egg (or 2 small ones)
1¾	cups cornmeal, yellow or white
1	cup milk
3	teaspoons baking powder
1	teaspoon salt
¼	teaspoon baking soda

Mother beat the egg, then mixed in the cornmeal and milk. Then she added the other ingredients and mixed it thoroughly.

She put the contents into muffin tins or pie pans for baking.

It usually baked in about 30 minutes in her oven on the kerosene stove.

She would serve us a dozen muffins or two pans of corn bread. We usually had a vegetable or two to go with the meal—often hominy made from our own corn, and french-fried potatoes. During the garden season we had fresh corn on the cob, tomatoes and any other vegetables we could raise.

Dad and his boys would come in from the field at noon, almost starving—or so the boys claimed. Mother always had the meal ready.

We sat down and devoured hot buttered corn bread, cool milk, hominy, and that delicious pot of beans with ham bits all through the bean gravy. The soup in those beans was delicious! The beans had cooked for about 4 hours over low heat, so they were soft and appetizing.

Often we'd put a slice of corn bread on our plates, then dip the beans out of the pot and spread them over the bread. It was quite tasty!

All those meals of corn bread and beans helped us make it through the bleak 1930s. We didn't have money, but we had faith and a purpose to survive. Corn bread and beans helped sustain us. ❖

The Champion of Churns

By Rosalind Lock

Must be a better way to do this," my brother grumbled as he stood at the kitchen table turning the wheel of our small glass churn. "With only a gallon of cream at a time, it's gonna take forever."

It had been a week since the dairy farmers began to refuse to ship milk unless they were better paid. In the meantime Dad fed the skimmed milk to the stock, but the cream for churning had accumulated.

Across the kitchen Mother was busy preparing to pack the butter into 1-pound molds, some with pretty designs and others simply plain wooden boxes.

She looked up when she heard my brother's complaint and watched him stretch his arms and flex his fingers.

"I think there may be a better way," she remarked. Then she walked directly to the small room where our washing machine stood. "Give me a hand to push this washer into the kitchen!" she called to us.

"Now what?" I asked my brother as we followed her.

"We're going to let the washer do the churning," she announced, tugging at the machine.

"This is a new one," my brother scoffed as we pushed the washer to center stage in the kitchen.

Mother removed the washer cover and scoured the inside with a vengeance. A country woman who long ago had learned to do two things at once, she plugged the machine in with

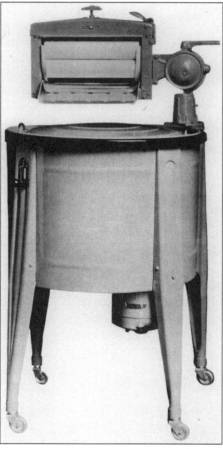

one hand and gestured toward the waiting pails of cream with the other.

"Pour it into the washer," she ordered.

With a little stretch of my imagination, I can still hear the cream splash as we emptied pailful after pailful into the washer's cavernous interior. Then, with the precision of a scientist conducting an experiment, Mother replaced the cover, flicked a switch and stood back.

There was a rhythmic slosh-slosh as the agitators swirled the cream around like a load of overalls.

Gradually the swishing diminished until, as if it could do more for the cause, the washer stopped.

The moment of truth had arrived. Mother flicked the switch off and removed the cover. Imagine our surprise when we peered into the machine and found ourselves staring at clumps of butter.

Mother smiled and nodded, as pleased as a person who wins a fortune with her first lottery ticket.

"Now what'll you do with so much butter at one time?" my brother asked as he resumed his place at the churn.

"Sell it," she replied, and began setting out more molds.

And sell it she did—to the neighbors, to the grocery store, and even to the dairy.

Today, when I push a grocery cart past the dairy case and see packages of butter arranged on the shelves, I am reminded of the time our washing machine doubled for a churn. ❖

Fruit of Their Labors

By Terry D. Wright

Green onions, turnips, carrots, lettuce, tomatoes, peppers and corn. These crops were how my great-grandfather, Isaac "Lovell" Wright, etched out a living during the Depression years.

Truck-patch farming was a popular livelihood during the Depression for many Midwesterners. This style of farming was characterized by strips of different kinds of produce growing on the same farm. And the crops grew plentifully in the rich soil of central Indiana. My great-grandfather gathered the ripe crops at least twice each week and sold them in Shelbyville.

Grandpa was a very familiar sight as he arrived with his white hair peeking out from under his old straw hat. He wore a blue shirt and bib overhauls; a corncob pipe was always in his mouth, but not often lit.

When Grandpa arrived at his daughter's home in Shelbyville, there was generally an argument as to which of the grandchildren would get to ride on the umbrella-covered wagon seat while Grandpa made his vegetable rounds.

The horse pulling Lovell's wagon was either Molly (perhaps named for his wife) or another ancient creature known for his blind eye. Those two horses were the strength of the entire farm. They helped with the plowing, planting and cultivating, and then helped sell the crops as they took their turns pulling the produce wagon on its rounds.

Once Lovell and one of the children were perched on the seat, the horse proceeded on its own, knowing the route full well. There were reins to guide the animal, but neither horse needed the help.

As he rode, Lovell would constantly call out, "Fresh vegetables! Fresh vegetables!" in a loud voice. Neighbors quickly surrounded the wagon to purchase from his hoard of goods.

The day of selling from the spring wagon wasn't finished until after supper at Grandpa and Grandma Wright's. Their old Gothic farmhouse sat on Camel Hill just a short distance from town. It was a welcome sight after a long day. The horse knew the way home and the weary merchant and grandchild could smell Grandma's cooking as they approached the house. There was always plenty to eat as Grandpa, Grandma and grandchild found their places around the table. All their food came from the farm. They had little material wealth, but they ate very well, despite the Depression.

During the Depression it wasn't unusual for people to barter for family needs. This was expressed in very practical terms one day when businessmen from "the big city" arrived at Lovell and Molly's farm.

The dignified representatives planned to build a mausoleum across from Lovell's farm. Because the men did not reside in the area, they wanted to "employ" Lovell to take care of the mausoleum and grounds. He was not to be paid cash, but he and his wife would have perpetual interment in the mausoleum.

Lovell diligently tended the spacious grounds and maintained the large, monumental building. Undoubtedly, he occasionally stopped during the course of labors to contemplate his final resting place and the final "rewards" he would earn for his efforts.

There was no other way this poor dirt farmer and his wife could have received the distinction of being entombed in a mausoleum. But they earned their place there, just as they had earned their livelihood—by the fruit of their labors. ❖

Grandmother The Brewer

By Harry S. Goodwin

Many folks find that beer or wine adds a cooling, refreshing touch and a lift to the spirits to meals and social hours. But my grandmother discovered long ago that a mug of homemade beer or a glass of wine—chilled in her only "refrigerator," the floor of her cool dirt cellar—lent zest to meals. And she knew nothing about ice cubes!

She did not know, as cooks do today, that wine gives a lift to many dishes when added during cooking. But she did know that a glass of her homemade wine or a mug of her home brew received a hearty welcome from Grandfather during a hot afternoon or at the evening table.

On those hot and humid days when water cannot quench my thirst, I recall how Grandmother satisfied hers. She didn't go to the corner store. Instead, she went down into her cool cellar and brought up cream-colored earthenware bottles of homemade sparkling ginger beer and, sometimes, other beers. Long before the hot weather set in, Grandmother made ginger beer and stored it away in her dirt-floored cellar. She used the same recipe year after year.

Her homemade wine or a mug of her home brew received a hearty welcome from Grandfather during a hot afternoon.

She had her wooden cask ready before she began to make the beer in her kitchen. Into a large tin pail she measured 2 pounds of brown sugar or 1 quart of molasses, 1½ ounces cream of tartar, and an equal amount of powdered gingerroot. She added 2 gallons of boiling water. She stirred it thoroughly to be sure all the ingredients were dissolved and blended before she poured it into the cask.

When the mixture had cooled to just milk-warm, she added a half-pint of potato yeast. Grandmother placed the wooden plug loosely in the bunghole so the brew could "work," or ferment. Then she shook the cask vigorously to make sure the yeast was mixed throughout the brew.

After 24 hours she strained the beer and bottled it. In 10 days the ginger beer was sparkling clear. Sometimes she sliced a lemon or two into it; then she called it lemon beer.

Grandmother made her own potato yeast. She always kept a cup or more on hand to use as starter for a new batch. Here is how I remember she made it: Grandmother pared 6 medium raw potatoes, then boiled them. Into the hot potatoes she mashed 6 large spoonfuls of wheat flour. Into the mixture she poured 2 pints of the boiling water in which the potatoes had cooked. She added 2 gills of sugar (a gill is ¼ cup) and a few dabs of salt.

When the mixture had cooled, she stirred in 2 gills of potato yeast. Sometimes she boiled a handful of home-grown hops in a quart of water for 10 minutes, then strained them and added the liquid to the potatoes.

Although ginger beer was our favorite, Grandmother sometimes delighted us with a mug of spruce beer. She made it by boiling a handful of hops and 2 handfuls of sassafras root chips in 10 gallons of water. When she thought the flavors of the hops and sassafras had saturated the water, she strained the mixture.

While it was still hot she added a gallon of blackstrap molasses and a few spoonfuls of spruce syrup (which she made by steeping 2 handfuls—or more—of fresh spruce tips until she had a thick liquid).

Then she added dabs of powdered gingerroot and 1 whole allspice berry, pounded fine. She poured it all into a wooden cask. When it was milk-warm, she added 2 gills of yeast, then plugged the bunghole loosely. When the beer had cleared and stopped working, she bottled it and corked the bottles tightly. This spruce beer was Grandmother's first choice for sipping on a scorching summer day. It refreshed and satisfied her family's thirst.

Grandmother enjoyed making wine even more—using a variety of berries, fruit and plants. Among other things, she made wine from parsnips, wild cherries, capers and rice. She also made wine from dandelion blossoms and elderberry blossoms, using these recipes:

Dandelion Blossom Wine

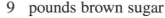

1	gallon boiling water
3	quarts dandelion blossoms
5	pounds brown sugar
	Juice and peel of 3 lemons
	Juice and peel of 3 oranges
2	gills potato yeast

Pour the boiling water over the dandelions. Let stand for 24 hours. Strain mixture; add brown sugar, the fruit juices, and the peels which have been cut in thin strips. Boil for 10 minutes and strain.

Let mixture cool until milk-warm, then add potato yeast. Pour into a crock and let stand until it begins to "work." Then bottle it, setting the corks loosely. After "working" (fermentation) stops, cork the bottles tightly.

Elderberry Blossom Wine

9	pounds brown sugar
3	gallons water
1	quart elderberry blossoms
2	gills potato yeast
3	pounds raisins

Mix brown sugar and water and bring it just to the boiling point, but do not boil. Add the elderberry blossoms, and let mixture cool until milk-warm. Then stir in potato yeast.

Place raisins in bottom of a crock; pour elderberry blossom mixture over raisins and let mixture stand in crock for 6 days, stirring it vigorously once each day.

Strain the wine into bottles, but do not cork. After wine stops working, cork bottles tightly.

Grandmother's recipe makes an excellent, clear, light-colored wine. Some people think it has a flavor like brandy. Others more correctly describe it as a cream sherry.

In my memory, I see Grandfather coming into the kitchen, slumping into his big chair by the table. Completely worn out, he pulls a red bandanna from his hip pocket and wipes his sweaty brow.

Grandmother fetches a mug of cool beer from the cellar and sets it on the table in front of him. Then she seats herself by his side and pats his hand. "Rest," she urges him. "No more in the cornfield this afternoon. The sky is leaden. A black cloud in the north threatens a heavy thundershower soon."

Swigging Grandmother's beers and sipping her wines are experiences that cannot be duplicated or bought in any package store—experiences which cannot be erased, but which can be relived only in memory. ❖

The Seed Catalog

By Virginia Hearn Machir

L ook, Maggie," said Father, his blue eyes sparkling as he turned the pages of our new seed catalog. It usually arrived at about the same time as the first January thaw. "Look at these zinnias, petunias, green peas and blood-red beets," he said to Mother. "I wish we could grow flowers and vegetables as pretty as the pictures in this book."

My parents would get as excited as a couple of kids on Christmas morning while they sat at the kitchen table and looked through the seed catalog, planning their spring and summer vegetable gardens.

The kerosene lamp burned in the center of the table as my parents dreamed over pictures of shiny red tomatoes, yellow onions and green cucumbers. My five sisters and I were seated around the table doing our homework, but we also tried to get a peek at the pictures in the catalog and put in our two cents' worth as to what we wanted to plant.

"We have plenty of seed potatoes left from last year's crop to use for planting. We won't have to buy seed potatoes," Father said. I remembered how we had cut the seed potatoes last year, leaving at least two eyes on each piece. Then we dropped the pieces in rows and covered them with soil.

We had planted the potatoes early on Good Friday and had raised a bumper crop. How much fun we had, digging the bushels and bushels of big brown potatoes! We stored them in bins in the root cellar, and all winter there was an ample supply for baked potatoes, mashed potatoes, hash browns and potato pancakes.

I also remember how we hated bugging the potatoes. We had to go down each row with a small switch and beat bugs off the vines and into a small bucket of kerosene. If we accidentally smashed one of the bugs on our skin, the next day a water blister would appear on the very spot. Mother called them potato bug blisters.

One of my sisters hated the task so much that she vowed that when she married she would buy all her potatoes at the grocery store so her children would never have to bug potatoes!

Mother turned another page in the catalog. "We want to have enough tomatoes to can this year," she said as she eyed the pictures of the big red beauties. "We should plant the seeds early in boxes indoors so they will be ready to set in the garden the first of May."

"Two packages of oxheart tomatoes," Father said as he wrote on the order blank, "and two packages of early cabbage seed. Do you think that's enough cabbage?"

"Yes, that's enough," Mother said, "but I want to be sure I have enough tomatoes for table use and canning and plenty of cabbage to cook, make slaw and kraut. Oh, and order some little yellow tomato seed. They make delicious preserves," she added, directing a teasing smile at Father.

One year, either Father had made an error in his order or the company had made a mistake when they sent our seeds. Father said he had ordered red tomato seed, but when the plants began bearing, they were all little yellow tomatoes.

You never saw so many in your life! We gave them to neighbors. Mother made dozens of jars of preserves. We fed them to the chickens and ate them ourselves until we felt like they were coming out of our ears!

The neighborhood men got to kidding Dad about his tomato crop. Whenever they saw him at the grocery or barbershop or blacksmith shop, one was sure to remark, "Dan, I hear you like little yellow tomatoes," or, "Dan, I hear you are fattening your pigs on little yellow tomatoes instead of corn." He became sort of touchy on the subject.

It had been several years since any little yellow tomatoes had been planted in our garden. "I'll order them if you're sure that's what you want," Father said, grinning sheep-

ishly. "How about cucumbers? Oh, yes, I want that early brand."

"That's the kind we planted last year, and remember how many pickles I canned," Mother said.

One of my sisters saw the picture of ornamental gourds. "Please, may we get some gourd seed to plant? Just for us?" she begged.

"Well, all right, but you can't plant gourds in the garden. Some people say they mix with pumpkins. You'll have to plant them to climb the trellis by the back porch," Mother told us.

"Oh, goody, goody! We get to have gourds! I'm going to paint some and hang a string in the kitchen," my sister said.

"I think I'll try peanuts again this year," Father said with an inquiring glance toward Mother.

"Now, why do you want to waste our money on peanut seed?" she asked. "You tried them last year and you didn't raise enough peanuts to feed a jay bird!"

Every year Father planted something different—purple pod beans, climbing strawberries or peanuts. They rarely produced much, but the pleasure we all derived from watching these novelties grow made up for the sparse harvest.

"Be sure and order some onion sets and sweet corn," Mother said.

"Corn on the cob is the *best* thing in the whole world I love to eat," my youngest sister chimed in.

Straight on through the seed catalog they turned pages and ordered seeds—spinach, cauliflower, swiss chard and popcorn.

"May we plant lots of popcorn?" I asked. I loved the big bowls of popcorn we popped in the wintertime and the popcorn balls we made at Christmastime.

They dreamed through the pictures of pumpkins and squashes, which took a lot of time, because when they planted, they had enough for the entire neighborhood. They

My parents would get as excited as a couple of kids on Christmas morning while they sat at the kitchen table and looked through the seed catalog.

1B CONVOLVULUS. (Morning Glory) Mixed
THE WEEKLY RECORDER. NEW YORK.

usually planted them in the cornfield because the pumpkin and squash vines covered so much territory. Once a vine grew out at the edge of the cornfield and climbed up into the lower branches of a tree where a large, crooked-neck cushaw squash hung from a limb.

This gave the neighborhood men something else to kid Dad about. Several of them came to

see the squash hanging from the limb of the tree and said, "Dan, if that tree grows any sprouts, save one for me, because I sure would like to have a squash tree."

Mother and Father planted nearly every variety of squash in the seed catalog—white scallop, green zucchini and gold necks for summer use, and, for winter, table queens, crooked-neck cushaws (which we stored in the root cellar) and lots of big orange pumpkins for pies

and jack-o'-lanterns to give to the neighbors.

The kerosene in the bowl of the lamp was nearly gone now, and Father and Mother were almost to the back of the seed catalog.

We five girls were getting sleepy, but we didn't want to miss a minute of ordering the seeds for our garden.

"Two packages of lettuce and two packages of radishes," Mother said as Father wrote it on the order. "And don't forget my flowers. Get mixed zinnias, dwarf marigolds and mixed petunias. That finishes our seed order for this year," Mother said as she closed the catalog.

I was glad she was going to plant flowers this year. I loved the long row of mixed red, yellow, pink and orange zinnias she had planted next to the fence in the garden so we could see them from the front yard.

The pink and white petunias she had planted by the front porch had been beautiful all summer.

I went to bed, remembering the great feeling of pride and accomplishment that had overcome me last fall when I went into the root cellar and viewed the shining glass jars of red tomatoes, green beans, sweet corn, beets, pickles, relish, golden peaches, yellow tomato preserves, jams, jellies and watermelon rind preserves standing in rows on the shelves.

Our garden was a family affair, for we children helped plant the seed, cultivate the growing plants, harvest the vegetables and prepare them for canning. What a marvelous learning experience it was for us!

Back in those days, we had never heard of "togetherness," but we had it—right there in our vegetable garden. ❖

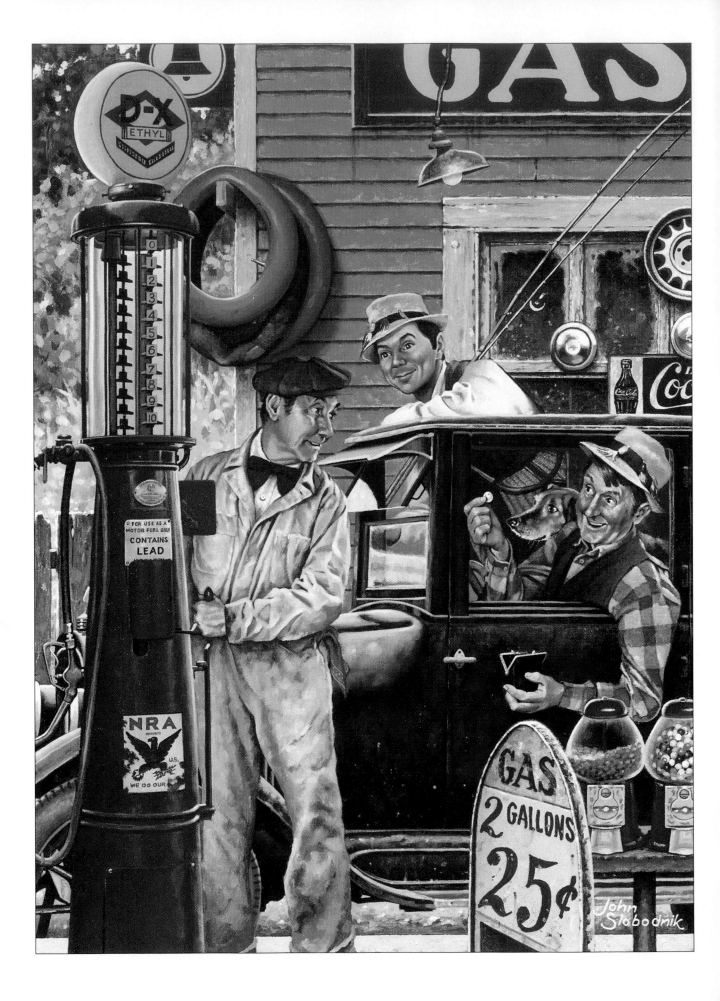

Pinching Pennies

As the editor of *Good Old Days*, I invariably get stories during the summer about berry picking. Like so many of our readers, my siblings and I made more than our share of trips to the briers and thickets to search out the juicy berries.

Sometimes the fruit of our labor was turned into some of Mama's delicious pies or cobblers. Mama always turned part of the harvest into jams and jellies for the breakfast table; she also canned a generous portion of the berries for our winter consumption.

But more often than not we three young entrepreneurs—Dennis, Donna and I—turned the berries into a little spending money, selling them by the quart and gallon to neighbors and passersby. As children who knew more than a little about pinching pennies, we could make our berry picking money—which literally seemed like a Godsend—last for what seemed like months of penny candy and pop. Maybe there would even be a Saturday movie matinee thrown in that bottomless berry pail.

I know of no job which doesn't have its perks—and its pitfalls. The perks of berry picking, obviously, was the money we made and the delicious fringe benefit of popping a fresh, juicy blackberry into our mouths whenever the desire struck us. The pitfalls—and what few seem to recall when remembering those berry picking days of old—were the ticks and chiggers. (Perhaps it is human nature to remember the good and block out the bad.) I believe for every penny's worth of berries, I picked up at least one of those parasitic pains in the posterior.

Berry picking forays always began with Daddy dusting the legs of my overalls with sulphur in an attempt to deter the ticks. We always had cattle in the fields with the best blackberry vines, so there seemed to be no end to the seed ticks and chiggers lurking on the long stems of grass, ready to be brushed onto an unsuspecting berry picker. I could tolerate lacerations of arm and hand in the thorny briers, especially when I thought of the monetary rewards awaiting, but a tick bite was sheer torture when you couldn't get to where the itch was (and there was plenty of biting and itching before the day was over).

Upon our return home, Mama made us shed clothes in the front yard and climb into the galvanized tub which had been awaiting us, warming in the summer sun. A quick bath and a thorough, motherly checkup insured that we were basically parasite free.

Maybe no one else had ticks and chiggers in their berry vines.

More likely, everyone did and now they just want to forget about it.

I like to remember because, like so many other parts of our youth, some of the sweetest memories have just a slight edge of pain—or at least an uncomfortable itch. We remember the simple joys of life—the love of family, friends and community. Still, those joys more often than not were tempered by illness, Depression and war. That's just the way life is.

Berry picking taught me early on in life a valuable lesson in self-sufficiency. Mama and Daddy didn't have money for many frills, so if we kids wanted something bad enough we figured out a way to earn it for ourselves, despite the pesky ticks.

I still like to go down into the hollow behind our house to pick blackberries and dewberries. I don't sell them now; I don't need the money like I did back then, and the sweetness of the fruit is much better than any pennies I might pinch from the sale.

I still like to keep an old cow; she still drops a few ticks and they still seem to find me. But when I feel that familiar itch I just smile, go for another handful of fruit and know that, like ticks in the berry patch of life, the pain of the moment will never overshadow the lessons learned berry picking in the Good Old Days.

—Ken Tate, Editor

Allowances: Who Needs 'Em?

By R.E. Strang

We boys hadn't heard of allowances for kids back around 1910. A kid either earned his own money or went without. In those days, youngsters were to be seen and never heard, unless spoken to. A place to sleep, three ample meals a day, a pair of overalls, a pair of shoes, a shirt, a once-a-week change of underwear, plus a clean shirt and a pair of knickers for Sunday—what else could a boy possibly need?

But back to money. We earned a few pennies, a nickel or a dime, or maybe a quarter here and there. When I was 8 or 9, a little old man (he seemed old to us; probably 40 or 45!) came to the apple orchard my father was managing. He was looking for apple buds to graft onto seedlings at the nursery he operated. The budded trees would be planted on farms later to become orchards. Going into our orchard, he clipped 8- to 12-inch twigs from selected trees.

We earned a few pennies, a nickel or a dime, or maybe a quarter here and there.

Now came my opportunity to earn a little money. The nurseryman became my employer. He provided me with a pair of clippers and instructed me on how to clip the leaves from the twigs he had gathered. I carefully clipped each leaf, leaving a quarter-inch stem on the twig at each bud.

For this I was paid 10 cents for every 100 twigs I defoliated. I could clip 100 twigs after school, and maybe as many as 300 or 400 on a Saturday. Thirty or 40 cents was unheard-of pay for a single day for any kid!

I later learned to make apple boxes from "shooks"—the wooden ends, side and bottom slats from which the old-fashioned wooden apple boxes were made. I earned a penny for every box I could nail together. At that rate, I could make 40 or 50 cents on a Saturday.

Another way to pick up pennies was to search the town dump for discards. A tote sack, gunnysack or potato sack—as burlap bags were called—was worth a penny if in good condition. A pint whiskey flask was worth nothing, but it could be exchanged for a free soda pop at the local bottler. Some liquor bottles were worth a penny when delivered to the bottler.

The best source of money from the dump was discarded medicine bottles. In those days, druggists cleaned and reused the bottles. We gathered them in a wooden box and took them to the drugstore. The druggist, whom I remember as a benevolent, bald gentleman, carefully marked down 1, 2 or sometimes 3 cents for each bottle, according to its type and size. Often our total would run to 25 or 50 cents; we felt quite affluent after a payoff at the drugstore.

Today, even the thought of kids digging around in a dump would raise questions of sanitation. But in those days, the town dump was probably much cleaner than today's city streets where kids play.

Kids could also make money picking fruit and berries. I picked apricots into half-bushel baskets for 5 cents per basket. It was amazing how many 'cots one of those baskets would hold. But it was far more amazing how long it took to make a nickel selling papers and magazines: *The Saturday Evening Post* sold for 5 cents—2 cents for the kid salesman.

Picking green beans was the most profitable work I did as a boy. We received 1 cent for every pound we picked. Most days we could make $1, give or take a few cents. On good picking days we might make as much as $2 or $3. These were bush beans. We bent over at the hips and picked beans from the low vines all day long. We were lucky if we could straighten up by the time we reached home at night.

I even went into the poultry business. I bought a pair of bantam chickens from a friend for 50 cents and purchased a large bag of feed for another 50 cents. The little hen laid eight eggs, which I carefully gathered and stored.

When she was ready to set, I returned her eggs to her. She faithfully sat on the eggs for the required 21 days and hatched seven healthy chicks. The little rooster strutted all over the yard, letting everyone know what a proud papa he was.

Soon after the chicks hatched, our family moved. I sold my little flock of banties for $1, so I realized no profit or loss from my first business venture. But though I received no pay for my labor, I did obtain some valuable experience. This was not to be the last deal from which experience was my only gain.

County fair prize money was another source of potential income for us kids. We exhibited squash, pumpkins, corn and other vegetables from our gardens. We also built birdhouses, tie holders, whatnot shelves, jewel boxes and any other items we could think of. First prize was $2 plus a blue ribbon; second prize was $1 and a red ribbon.

One summer I built an elaborate set of miniature furniture. I exhibited it in two orange crates which I'd covered and decorated to represent four tiny rooms—a living room, dining room and two bedrooms. The fair management informed me that they had no prize they deemed appropriate for my project, but I was offered the privilege of an all-expenses-paid trip to the state fair at Salem. I went with a group from our county who put on a play at the fair.

For one week, we had a wonderful time at the state fair. All the boys were billeted with an Army company that had set up camp on the fairgrounds to police the fair. We were each issued a mess kit, and we stood in line for our meals at the Army mess. We slept in a large tent with a big wood-burning stove in the center.

I graduated from grammar school the following spring, and the next fall our family moved to a farm in a remote area near Portland. We had no bicycles. We walked where we wanted to go, or rode in our horse-drawn hack.

But in Portland, it seemed that every kid had a bicycle. One neighborhood bike shop had a sale—brand-new, double-bar bikes for $38. By now I had about $40 in my own bank account. In a moment of weakness I spent practically all my life savings on the blue bike that caught my eye. It was my first large investment—and a dream come true. Now I had wheels! ❖

> *Kids could make money picking fruit and berries. I picked apricots into half-bushel baskets for 5 cents per basket.*

Our Little Nest Egg

By Helen M. Peterson

Simply impossible!" I heard one lady tell another more than a few years ago. "It is simply impossible to save money these days! Everything costs so much!"

She told about giving her children modest allowances. Her 4-year-old received 50 cents a week; the three school-age youngsters each got $1. I listened to the two young mothers discussing the issue, but my thoughts drifted back to when money was scarce indeed, and the only way we could build up a "little nest egg" was to save one penny at a time.

During the Depression, Father's income was very meager. Every cent was desperately needed to buy necessities for everyday living, yet Mother insisted we must save something for a rainy day—a day when an emergency might arise and we would need cash to meet the situation. We were encouraged to eke out a penny, a nickel or a dime whenever we could and store it away in a little tin cup.

Mother let us take turns dropping coins in the cup. We all kept track of the money. Pennies were exchanged for dimes, dimes for dollars, and eventually—very slowly—dollar bills turned into fives.

When emergencies arose—and they did, as they do in all households—that money came in mighty handy, like the time brother Donnie fell and skinned his knee coming home from school. Normally Mom would clean the injury with alcohol and bandage it with a sterile dressing, and the wound would heal without complications. But Donnie's knee didn't heal. Infection set in.

The doctor bill plus medications came to over $60, and we were all glad our nest egg had enough money to meet the obligation.

Mostly the unexpected emergencies were illnesses of some kind, but there were situations

which called for a family council to decide whether or not the situation was important enough to merit digging into our nest egg.

I remember the day Rosie came home and said, "Mom, I won first in the 'declam contest' today, and I'm eligible to enter the regional contest." There was no dissent among the family about taking the needed cash from the tin cup to pay for Rosie's lunch and bus fare to go to the nearby city; it didn't cost much.

And when Rosie won the regional and was eligible for the district contest 70 miles distant, all agreed that the few dollars needed to cover expenses could be taken again from the nest egg.

When Rosie came home from the district contest wearing the blue ribbon and stated she could now enter the state contest, we were very proud of her indeed.

Although the state contest was to be held 300 miles away, Rosie's expenses would be quite nominal, for contestants were given special rates for transportation and lodging. There was no question of where the money would come from. This was an emergency— and we had saved for it.

But two days before her departure, Rosie came home from school in tears. She had heard that all the other contestants were being accompanied by their mothers.

This was the first time our little nest egg was emptied to meet an emergency other than sickness. When Mother and Rosie returned from the state contest and we learned Rosie had won again, we were all very proud that we, in a small way, had been a part of it.

Many times over the years our coffer was emptied, and temporarily our feeling of security would wane. But we always started right over again saving our pennies so that we'd have a nest egg when the next emergency arose. ❖

10-Cent Date

By J.B. Cearley

We lived smack-dab in the middle of nowhere. Tommy Davis' folks were were like mine—sandy-land cotton farmers on the high plains of West Texas. Our dry farms sat in the middle of a triangle of towns, 16 miles to each. Old Sol was blinking in the west, ready to squat for the night, when I heard Tommy's old Model A Ford rattle to a stop out front. We had plans to drive to town to see some girls and take in a good movie that Saturday night in September 1934.

"Ready to go?" Tommy asked.

"And rarin'. Think we can find those girls?"

"Sure. Carol has a date for you. I think her name is Robin Snider. Real cute girl, Carol said."

Tommy gunned the old motor. The car lurched forward, and we went bouncing along the dusty road. A moment later, Tommy said, "I hope you've got money for gas. The tank is near empty. And I'm almost broke. Got 80 cents."

> *"I hope you've got money for gas. The tank is near empty. And I'm almost broke. Got 80 cents."*

"I've got gas up at the west corner of our field," I told him. "I only have 60 cents."

He seemed incredulous. "Gas in the field?"

"Sure." He drove on for 200 yards, then I pointed to a cedar post in our fence. "It's there. In the weeds by the fence." I got out and walked into our maize field where I had hidden a 3-gallon can of gasoline.

I put the gas in the car. Then we started for town and some excitement after a week of hard work. Tommy suddenly looked at me to ask, "Where'd you get the gas?"

"County grader stopped for the night not far on the other side of our house. The grader cheerfully donated the gas."

"Good old county graders," Tommy said. "Only place a poor boy can find cheap gasoline." Darkness settled over the plains, so Tommy snapped on the headlights.

We turned a corner and headed west for a mile. The road came to a dead end and we had to make a square right turn to the north. A minute later the lights began to blink on and off. Then they went out completely. "We must be near the corner," Tommy said. He had the Ford moving rapidly.

Suddenly the car lurched and leaped into the air as the wheels hit a ditch. Our heads banged into the ceiling as dust flew in the old sedan. The car bounced across the ditch and into a cornfield. "Don't let her stop!" I advised. "We'll never get out of here if you stop in the field."

Tommy shifted into low gear and gunned the motor as we spun around and lurched back onto the roadway. "We got to have a little light," he said. We barely could make out the roadway.

I got out and raised the hood. Feeling along the wires in the dim moonlight, I found a place where the wire had no insulation. I tied the wire so it could not touch metal and short the lights. Then I took some tinfoil from a gum wrapper and wound it around the blown fuse, replaced it, and the lights came on.

"Let's go," Tommy complained. "It's 7 more miles."

When we got to town, Tommy drove down to where his girl's family lived. Robin was at Carol's house, and the girls were waiting for us anxiously. Robin proved to be cute indeed, with dark brown hair and brown eyes. I liked the way she had arranged her long dark curls around her face.

We walked to the car and I asked, "Is there a good movie showing tonight?"

Carol offered, "There's a good movie that Robin and I want to see at the State Theater. Will Rogers is playing in it."

"Sounds great," I agreed.

The admission price was 10 cents each. After we got the tickets, I bought two Baby Ruth candy bars for me and Robin; another dime gone.

The movie was delightfully funny, but it was even more thrilling to sit by a pretty girl and hold her hand. I felt like I had been transported to some magical place.

After the movie we were walking to the car,

which we'd parked a block away. As we passed a small café I saw a new sign in the window: "Hot Texas Chili, 10 cents."

I still had 30 cents, enough for chili and coffee for me and Robin. "Let's have a treat of a bowl of that chili," I suggested.

They all agreed, so we went inside and ordered chili and coffee. We all felt like big shots, sitting there in the dim light of the restaurant, eating hot chili and crackers and sipping coffee. It was a real treat for a country boy on a date.

All good things end, and we finally had to walk back to the car. As I turned to open the door for Robin, I saw something that looked like a washer lying on the pavement. After Robin got into the car, I bent to pick it up. It was a half-dollar. I was rich again!

We drove to Robin's home, and I walked her to the door.

"May I have another date?" I asked.

She played it coy. "Well, perhaps."

"Next Saturday night?"

"That might be all right," she said.

We arrived at the front porch. "How about a little kiss?" I asked softly.

"My mother probably is watching," she whispered. "Thanks for the movie and treats. You seem like a nice boy." Then she turned, gave me a kiss, and disappeared into her house.

When I got back into the Ford, I had trouble climbing down to get into the thing. I was walking 3 feet above the ground!

Tommy and I started the long trip back home. We were tired and quiet, thinking about the movie and the girls. I was happy that the lights worked all the way home. I was tired and happy. I had another date with that cute girl, saw a classy movie, had chili and coffee, got a sweet kiss, and I was only out 10 cents since I'd found that half-dollar. Not a bad night! ❖

My Unforgettable Christmas Transaction

By Mary Maniaci Pulcino

It was a typical December night for New York City, a couple of days before Christmas. Snow fell gently, transforming our East Harlem tenements into a fairyland.

I was the next-to-youngest of nine children, and felt pretty much out of the Christmas spirit because we were not going to have a tree. It was 1940. Times were hard, money was short and Christmas trees a luxury. Although I was only 9 years old, I took it upon myself to shop around for a tree.

Wrapped in my warmest clothes, I took my equally well-wrapped sister Margaret, who was all of 7, with me.

At our local produce store, owned by a nice Italian man called Patsy, we found several trees on wooden stands. All of them towered over Margaret and me.

"Hi, Patsy. How are things going?"

"Hello, girls," Patsy replied. "What can I help you with?"

"We were looking at your trees."

"Oh, I got lots of beautiful ones. Which one you like?"

I gulped and looked at little Margaret, so small and thin, her big blue eyes looking quizzically at me. Oh boy, I thought, how stupid I am! How is this going to work out?

I swallowed hard. We'd gone this far; we might as well go all the way.

"Margaret, you like this one?" I asked. It was a gigantic evergreen—the biggest, fullest tree I'd ever seen.

"Oh, yes!" Margaret said, her cheeks rosy and her face glowing joyously.

"We'd like this one, Patsy, but—" I could barely look him in the eye.

"Whatsa matter, Mary? It's too big for you two to carry?"

"Oh, no! We can carry it. Right, Margaret?"

"Yes, yes!"

"Then whatsa matter?"

"We only have a quarter—25 cents."

"Fine! Justa what it costs! It's all yours!"

"You mean it? Really? For sure? Oh, Patsy!" we shouted. "Thanks! Thanks! Merry Christmas! *Buon Natale*, Patsy!" I quickly handed him the quarter.

"Merry Christmas, girls," he answered, a twinkle in his eyes.

Margaret and I carefully wrapped our arms around opposite ends of the beautiful tree, just managing to keep it off the ground. Walking slowly and carefully and stopping every few feet to adjust our grip, we managed to carry that tree the block-and-a-half home.

Leaving it outside our apartment building, we entered the hallway on the ground floor. Our parents and most of our older brothers and sisters were in our apartment. We didn't want to leave the tree alone, and we were too exhausted to run up the flight of stairs, so we shouted up the stairs, calling our brothers to come help us.

Out they came, and down the stairs. "What's going on, you two? A tree! How on earth?"

"Only a quarter! Patsy let us have it for only 25 cents! Isn't it beautiful?"

And beautiful it was. It touched our dining room ceiling and filled the room with an elegance and majesty befitting the grandest of homes. Its pine scent was ever present that memorable holiday, and turned our modest apartment into a Christmas fantasyland. ❖

Swapping & Trading

By Vernon Brown

I am the world's worst swapper. Swapping and trading is rapidly becoming a lost art in the United States, but it was not so long ago that many people made a living for themselves and their families by shrewd trades.

My father, Tom Brown of Broken Arrow, Okla., was one of the old line of Arkansas swappers. He was raised in the Arkansas hills near the little community of Ash Flat, which is a few miles south of Salem. During the early days of Oklahoma statehood, there was a mass exodus of Ash Flatters to Oklahoma. Most of them, including Dad, settled in and near Coweta.

Dad continued to swap, swapping land, cattle, automobiles and trucks, homes and clothes. During my childhood, Dad would order handbills printed every six months and hold an auction and sell everything on the place. The cow, furniture, setting hens—every-thing went except Mother's sewing machine, which was "taboo." Then we moved to another house—usually rented— and Dad started to get ready for the next option or swap-out.

One day during the Depression Dad advertised that he would hold "A Public Auction of Cattle and Horses" behind Mr. Ferris' store in Coweta. He didn't have any horses or cattle himself, but he spread the word among farmers that he would auction off stock to the highest bidder for the fee of $1 per head.

I remember watching Dad that day, and I was so proud of him. His auctioneer's chant was melodious to my young ears.

One gawky farmboy had brought an old gray sway-backed mare to the sale. She looked like she was long past due for the glue factory. Finally they ran the old mare into the ring and Dad started chanting his unintelligible plea.

He tried and tried, and spent 20 minutes more on that sale than he had on the others. But all he could get was a $1 bid.

The farmboy's face got redder and redder and pretty soon his Adam's apple started bobbing up and down his skinny throat. I'll bet he and I were thinking the same thing: *What happens to the dollar?* Dad's fee was $1—and he had to sell to the highest bidder.

I watched Dad after the sale to see what he would do. He called the boy over. "Here, boy," he said, "this dollar is your Christmas present."

Like I said, I'm the world's worst trader. When I was 12, Dad traded for several used cars. One was a Model T Ford roadster which sat in the yard for several days. One day I asked him what he intended to do with it. He looked down at me. "You can have it," he said.

I couldn't drive, but my friend Odell Miller could, so I looked him up, and we took "the bug" out for a spin. Odell said, "What will you take for this car?"

I hesitated like Dad always did, chewed on an imaginary cud of tobacco for a while, spit and said, "What have you got to trade on?"

Well, I traded that car to Odell for a little hand-operated motion-picture projector and three 25-foot rolls of film starring Fatty Arbuckle. Later I let the projector and film go for a $1 watch and a knife that they handed out at Hunsecker's General Merchandise Store with each purchase of Poll Parrot shoes.

Two weeks later Dad took me down to my Uncle Willie's farm near Coweta. My cousin had been picking up hickory nuts and walnuts. I traded the watch and knife for 200 pounds of hickory nuts and 100 pounds of walnuts.

Dad never said a word during any of these transactions, but sometimes I would catch him looking at me—and it might have been my imagination, but it seemed like there was a slight smile on his face. ❖

> *Dad would order handbills printed every six months and hold an auction and sell everything on the place.*

Our First Car

By Virginia Hearn Machir

My father's first car was a 1917 Model T which he purchased in 1922. It came equipped with skinny tires, isinglass curtains we snapped on when it rained, a horn that went *Oo-oogah! Oo-oogah!* and a hand crank which was used to start the motor. My sisters and I were as proud of it as if it had been a Rolls Royce.

Father had never driven an automobile before, and on our first few trips, no one was permitted to talk as it distracted him from his driving. If my sisters or I forgot and talked, he would roar from the front seat, "Shut up! I can't drive with all that noise!"

One time when he approached the slat gate into our lane, instead of pushing on the brake pedal he just pulled back on the steering wheel and yelled "Whoa! Whoa!" The Model T went right through the gate and broke the latch, but pushed the gate open without damaging the gate itself. "Dan," Mom asked, "did you think you were driving a team of mules?"

But Dad soon learned the knack of navigating the Ford, even while we had conversation.

Mother learned to drive too, but she was never very good in reverse. Once when she backed the Model T out of the garage, she forgot to apply the brake at the top of the hill—and the car rolled down the hill and hit a peach tree, breaking both the tree and a taillight. At least the collision stopped its descent! Father never tired of telling how Mother not only broke the car's taillight, but also ruined his peach tree.

Our Model T gave us a jolting ride. The tires used high air pressure—it had to be 40 to 60 pounds to make them firm enough to carry the weight of the car. But being so hard, they did not offer a very comfortable ride.

We didn't have bumper stickers back then, but teen-age owners of Model T's painted signs on the bodies of their cars.

Every tire had a rubber inner tube which held the air. Occasionally as Father was driving along the gravel road, we'd hear a loud Pop!

"Another blowout!" Father would exclaim as he pulled off the highway to fix the flat. He repaired the tube by gluing a small rubber patch over the hole. Woe be to the motorist who forgot to carry the little kit containing those patches!

We didn't have bumper stickers then, but teen-age owners of Model T's painted signs on the bodies of their cars. Some of the signs we saw included:

"The Tin You Love to Touch"

"Peaches, Here's Your Can"

"T For Two"

"I Do Not Choose to Run"

"Danger: High Joltage"

"Barnum Was Right!"

"Here's Mud in Your Eye"

"Don't Laugh, Girls, Think How You Would Look Without Paint!"

We wanted Father to paint some signs on our Model T but he wouldn't hear of it.

We saw Model T's filled to capacity with teen-agers, with the overflow riding on the fenders. Roadsters with their tops down often carried a fellow and his date in the front seat and another pair of lovers in the rumble seat in back. This led preachers of the 1920s to expound on the evils of Mr. Ford's invention, declaring that those young people were surely going to hell in a Ford.

Regardless of the jokes made about the Model T, it was the most famous and popular car in automobile history. Our Model T took us on many happy trips to Grandma's, silent movies, county fairs and family outings. I'm glad I lived in the '20s and '30s and had the experience of riding in a Model T. ❖

Dearer Than Gold: Ration Stamp Book

By Marge Waterfield

Which treasure was more precious than money in 1943? That's right—the ration stamp book!

During the critical years of World War II, the government set up a rationing program to enable every family to obtain its share of the items that had been made scarce by war production. Itemizing all these products would be impossible here; just about everything from food to clothing and gasoline was scarce—and rationed.

The ration booklets were dispensed from centers set up in schools and voting booths. Each member of the family received his own book. The slogan "If you don't need it, don't buy it!" was printed on the booklet's back cover.

Those who complained about the long lines they waited in to get their stamps were in for a big surprise. They would stand in even longer lines trying to use the stamps.

I think we missed the rationed food items most. I remember trying to make fudge without sugar but it just didn't work. When our neighborhood store got some tiny, ½-ounce cans of pepper, my sister and I stood in line for hours.

Butter had also gone to war, and oleo found its way onto tables that had never seen it before. The scarcity of chocolate and coffee changed many menus.

It was not uncommon for stores to advertise horse meat for sale, but even that took ration stamps.

276|418 U

UNITED STATES OF AMERICA
OFFICE OF PRICE ADMINISTRATION

WAR RATION BOOK FOUR

Issued to ....
(Print first, middle, and last names)

Complete address ....

....

READ BEFORE SIGNING

In accepting this book, I recognize that it remains the property of the United States Government. I will use it only in the manner and for the purposes authorized by the Office of Price Administration.

Void if Altered ....
(Signature)

It is a criminal offense to violate rationing regulations.

OPA Form R-145　　　　　　　　　　　　　　　　16—35570-1

Above: The front cover of a War Ration Book, issued by the Office of Price Administration. The book is part of the editor's memorabilia from the war years. Right: The back of the same book. Note the admonition to recycle for "munitions for our fighting men" and to "cooperate with your local Salvage Committee."

NEVER BUY RATIONED GOODS
WITHOUT RATION STAMPS

NEVER PAY MORE THAN THE LEGAL PRICE

United States Office of Price Administration

IMPORTANT: When you have used your ration, salvage the TIN CANS and WASTE FATS. They are needed to make munitions for our fighting men. Cooperate with your local Salvage Committee.

☆ U. S. GOVERNMENT PRINTING OFFICE : 1943　16—35570-1

An announcement of a shipment of "rayons" would bring the women to a store by the thousands. Although it was usually a fight to the finish, the hose were sad imitations of the silk hosiery women had worn before the war.

Many women resorted to painting their legs with an orangish-brown liquid which was supposed to resemble stockings. The only improvement it had over rayons was that it didn't sag or snag.

Because cigarettes were so hard to get, my grandfather rolled his own. I was terribly impressed by the tiny roller machine he used.

When he licked the edge of the thin paper and rolled the cigarette into shape, I thought he was a genius. I often wondered why he took the bus clear across town when he heard that a certain store had a shipment of cigarettes for sale. I thought it looked like more fun to roll your own.

As if ration stamps weren't complicated enough, the government added points, tokens and cat stickers to the program. As we cautiously counted each stamp and token spent, it sometimes became more complicated than the Bank of America.

Most families traded stamps with one another for items they needed more.

Sometimes a neighbor needed a sugar coupon and we needed more coffee, so the trading went on and on.

You were given a Class A, B or C gasoline sticker to put on the windshield, depending on how far you had to drive to work. Dad was lucky; he could walk to work. So we saved our gas for weekend trips to the lake.

Once on the road, however, we worried constantly about whether the tires would hold up. No amount of stamps or cash could buy a decent tire. When all else failed, worn-out tires were recapped. This was like covering the tire with a thin layer of mucilage.

As we drove along, we often saw parts of recapped tires lying by the side of road where they had parted company.

By no means am I implying that those were the "good old days." They were filled with the horrors of war. But even wartime had its own special memories.

Do you remember these from 1943?

Teen-agers danced the jitterbug.

Girls swooned over a new singer named Frank Sinatra.

Every jukebox blared The Andrews Sisters singing *Rum and Coca-Cola* or *Praise the Lord and Pass the Ammunition*.

Every neighborhood had its own air-raid warden.

Letters from servicemen were called V-Mail.

Movie stars held Bond Rallies in every major city. Every back yard contained a Victory Garden. Everyone listened to *Hit Parade* on Saturday night.

"The slip of a lip can sink a ship" and "V for victory" were common expressions among us as schoolchildren.

As children, we kept busy while being patriotic in many ways. We saved tin cans and stamped them flat. On certain days we piled them out by the curb, and they were picked up by men in big trucks.

We saved all our used grease and returned it to the local butcher for 2 cents a pound. We tied our old newspapers in large bundles and sold them during the big paper drives.

I never quite understood how the cans and grease and newspapers helped us win the war, but I never regretted helping.

Fortunately, our children do not have to scrimp and save and go without—but they will never have the memories of those precious little stamps! ❖

The Potato Caper

By Pearl Chadwell

Late one summer in the early 1900s, my aunt told her husband, my Uncle Harry, that it was time to lay in the family's winter supply of potatoes.

Now, Uncle Harry was neither a farmer nor a gardener. The only time he ever got dirt under his fingernails was when he picked up a dime or nickel off the street. Not only didn't he farm or garden; Uncle Harry was so tight he squeaked when he walked.

He didn't look forward to buying the 30 to 50 bushels of potatoes it would take to get his family of seven through the coming year. Stingy as he was, potatoes formed the main part of practically every meal.

Then he had an inspiration that bordered on genius. He ran an ad in the local paper, and had some fliers printed up and distributed. Some were nailed to posts and trees; others were placed in public windows. He gave the rest to his children to hand out to anyone who would take one.

His announcement read: "Potato Contest! Send half a peck of potatoes to the address printed below for judging. The potatoes become the property of the sponsor of the contest. First prize $25; second prize $10; third prize $5."

Uncle Harry lived in a suburban area where anyone who could put his spade in the ground three times without hitting a fence had a garden, and 99 percent of these gardeners grew potatoes as their main crop. Potatoes started

rolling in like manna from heaven. Soon the basement was full, the garage was full, and the overflow started to take over the living room. Each half-peck of potatoes was kept carefully separate with the name and address of the sender, and that took a lot of room.

My aunt was very happy when the deadline for entering the contest approached. As the date drew nearer, the entries increased. My aunt envisioned her bedrooms and kitchen overflowing with spuds. In fact, she even had nightmares in which potatoes sprouted tiny arms and legs and advanced against her family, waving potato mashers and ordering them out of the house as the potatoes took over.

Uncle Harry then called an expert to judge the entries and award the prizes. Uncle Harry's expenses included $10 for advertising, $40 in prizes, and $10 for the judge's fee. For 200 bushels of potatoes, his total cost was $60!

He didn't feel the least bit of remorse when he advertised those prime, Grade A potatoes for sale at $2 per bushel. He sold 150 bushels with no trouble, grossing $300 for himself.

After deducting the expenses from the contest, he'd netted his family $240—and a plentiful supply of prime, Grade A potatoes, the best money could buy!

After the neighbors learned all the facts, they agreed on one thing: Uncle Harry wasn't as stupid as he looked. ❖

Bottles & Baskets of Fuel

By Virginia Petroplus Killough

My Depression childhood, in a small, personal way, was my first experience with an energy crisis. It happened to me, as it happened to many others, back in the 1930s.

One day the electric bill came. Mama, calmly ignoring it, brought up an old kerosene lamp from the basement. What had been a sentimental reminder of her early life in the country was about to be restored to a useful life.

I was given a nickel and a quart milk bottle and instructions to buy 5 cents' worth of kerosene from the corner gas station.

When the electricity was shut off a few days later, we were ready.

Of course, we missed the radio, but there were always books from the library. Some of my happiest memories are of the six of us sitting around the kitchen table, some reading, some playing checkers or a quiet game of dominoes in the warm glow of that kerosene lamp.

Hot water? There was the teakettle. Baths? Saturday night only. Refrigeration? We didn't even have an icebox at that time, so that was the least of our worries. Mama kept the milk and butter on the icy back porch all winter. In summer we bought only what we could use before it could spoil.

Soon after this, the gas bill came. It too was an impossible hurdle. Daddy went out and brought home our stove for the duration—a long, three-burner kerosene model with a separate little tin oven to perch on top. At times this stove gave off a terrible odor, but it was a source of heat, and we had macaroni and lentils and homemade bread in winter, and in the summer, green bean stew from the garden. The cooking problem was solved.

For heat we still had the old coal furnace. We closed off three enclosed porches to conserve our small coal supply. I know now that that dwindling pile of coal must have been a nightmare to my father on cold January nights.

About this time, he developed what I thought was a rather peculiar habit. He would put a bushel basket on my sister's wagon and walk down to a certain spot on the nearby railroad tracks where odd pieces of coal were sometimes scattered about. When he came home the bushel basket was full of beautiful, hard, shiny coal, patiently gathered piece by piece.

Even then it had a jewel-like quality to me—like black emeralds. That was how our father kept us warm.

We were "within walking distance" of everything—school, the park, the forest preserve, the library and church. It was 5 miles to the zoo, and 5 miles back.

Of course, we had long since put the car away safely in the garage. It had not been driven for months. Daddy put it up on blocks to save the tires, and we walked.

We were "within walking distance" of everything—school, the park, the forest preserve, the library and church. It was 5 miles to the zoo, and 5 miles back. We walked.

In particular, I remember spending Thanksgiving with our dearest friends, who lived far, far away on the other side of town. I remember the warm welcome, the fun and laughter, the pumpkin pie Mama carried over, the feasting, and the walk home, the six of us all together in the darkness, moving contentedly and quietly through the soft flakes of the first snowfall of that enchanted year.

I suppose these simple ways of facing a crisis are beyond reach of most of us these days. But once upon a time, that was the way it was. ❖

John
Slobodnik

College the Hard Way

By Oliver E. Rooker

As I approached graduation Grandma and I often discussed my chances of going to college after high school. "I won't be able to help you financially," she said, "but I will help you any other way I can." It was 1935. We were at the bottom of the Great Depression, and money was unbelievably scarce.

"We had a good garden this year. There are over 400 jars of canned fruits, vegetables and jelly in the cellar. The potato crop was extra good, so you will have to eat lots of potatoes.

"I canned 36 quarts of currants this summer. You could take a currant pie back with you each week if you could carry it in your grip. The only canned meat we have is the rabbit I canned two years ago."

Oh, yes—the rabbit. That winter of '33 it snowed so much that the wild rabbits couldn't run. My brother and I would go out with sticks (there was no money for shells) and get 10 to 20 rabbits a day. The temperature stayed near freezing for six weeks, and by then we had more than 100 frozen rabbits hanging in our screened-in back porch.

That same year there had also been an overabundance of wild plums, which Grandma canned. Consequently, for what seemed like a year, it was fried rabbit and stewed plums for breakfast, rabbit patties with plum jelly for dinner, and baked rabbit with plum butter for supper. For me, canned rabbit held no appeal.

"Also," Grandma continued, "when you come home each weekend, bring your dirty clothes and I'll have them washed and ironed by the time you are ready to go back."

Southwestern State Teachers' College in Weatherford, Okla., was 40 miles from our home in Canton. I had no car but had hitchhiked there several times; it usually took about an hour to get there.

The week before school started I went to Weatherford to enroll and rent a place to live. I rented a light housekeeping apartment—parlor, living room, kitchen and bedroom, all condensed within a 14- by 16-

> *"I won't be able to help you financially," she said, "but I will help you any other way I can." We were at the bottom of the Great Depression, and money was unbelievably scarce.*

foot room in the attic of a two-story house. The rent, $1 a week, was to be paid in advance; all utilities were furnished.

Bill Meeler was the proprietor of this boys' rooming house, and he went out of his way to help "his boys" in every way he could and still be a strict disciplinarian. "The college makes the rules for all student rooming houses, and I strictly enforce them. No alcoholic beverages of any kind on the premises, no girls past the front sitting room on the first floor, and I have added a couple more: No smoking in bed, and no radio playing or loud noises after 10 p.m."

Then he added, with special emphasis, "The first infraction I forget; the second one, you have to get out." The semester I was there, there were several violations, but no boys were forced to leave.

The day I left home to enroll, I was walking with a large suitcase in each hand. In my suitcases I was carrying a peck of small potatoes, 10 pints of home-canned vegetables, two onions, two cantaloupes, two pans, a skillet, a half-pint of lard, a shaker of salt, a dozen eggs, my clothes and a cotton-picking sack. With a load like that I didn't do much walking, but I was lucky that day. A car stopped and the driver took me to within six blocks of the rooming house.

I arrived at college with $34, my summer wages. After enrolling on Monday and buying my used books, I had $19.35 left to last me until I could find a job.

I went downtown—the college was "on the hill"—and bought eight cases of canned food. The 6-ounce cans sold for 5 cents each, or I could buy a case of 24 cans for $1. I bought a case each of black-eyed peas, butter beans, spaghetti and ravioli and four cases of soup for $8.

I now had $11 left, so I paid another five weeks' rent, leaving me $6 until I found a job.

When I'd first come to see about enrolling, I had applied for work with the National Youth Administration (NYA), a youth program designed to help students stay in school.

The fourth week I was there I received notice that my application had been approved. I was to report for work the next Monday afternoon. I had scheduled all my classes in the mornings and planned to pick cotton every afternoon and some weekends.

Now I had a job!

I didn't wait until Monday. I went right to the office and was told I could work up to 30 hours a month at 35 cents per hour—$10.50 per month. They let me work four hours a day, two days a week.

That first week we hauled fertilizer from the city sewer treatment plant a mile southeast of town and spread it on the football field. Later we did yard work around the campus and planted shrubs.

Each weekend I'd hitchhike home with my dirty clothes and empty fruit jars. I'd return to college with clean clothes, a loaf of homemade bread, a dozen eggs and a peck of potatoes.

Twice I hiked to Bridgeport 7 miles east and caught the 2 o'clock freight train to Eagle City, which was 7 miles from home; but the fare was 35 cents to ride in the caboose, and on $10.50 a month I couldn't afford the luxury.

Grandma said later that I had eaten more than 2 bushels of potatoes that semester. Potatoes were my main dish every day—boiled, mashed, mixed with a 5-cent can of potted meat or an egg or both, then fried. Even today I like this "main dish."

The last day of the semester was extremely cold. I left college and walked to the edge of town. Just as I thought I would freeze to death, I caught a ride to Eagle City. The first vehicle to come along was a farm tractor pulling a four-wheel trailer with a load of cotton tied down and covered with a tarp.

"Crawl up on top," the driver said. "I'm going to the gin in Canton."

I never thought I could get colder than I was then, so I climbed aboard. The man driving the tractor was dressed for this subfreezing weather. I wasn't. That was the longest 7 miles I ever traveled. He went right past my house, but I was too near frozen to tell him to stop.

At the gin it took two men to get me down from the trailer. One of them took me home,

and Grandma called our family doctor. After he examined me, he told Grandma, "I don't know what it is now, but Oliver has something besides being half-frozen. I don't think he will get any better tonight, but if he gets any worse, call me. Keep him in bed, and by morning we should know his ailment. Right now he is one sick boy."

The next morning we got the verdict: scarlet fever. The house, with Grandma and me inside, was quarantined for six weeks.

My brother, a high-school senior, lived with a neighbor during the quarantine. He could bring us our mail and groceries and leave them on the back porch, but he couldn't come in.

I never had a cold from that freezing ride but I was in bed for several days with the fever. During the next five weeks I felt good and helped Grandma cut blocks and tie four quilts. My wife and I still have one of those quilts I helped Grandma put together so long ago. ❖

Remember when folks used just about every method imaginable to save money? Every piece of material available was used for building or repair work. This fellow had the bright idea to use license plates to provide a fix for a leaking roof back in the days when metal was an expensive commodity.

The Versatile Hearse

By Nelson Pierce

My partner and I bought a sawmill near Colville in northeastern Washington and began operating it during the Depression, in 1934. We were interested in purchasing a small mill to cut railroad cross ties. Ties were selling great at the time—35 cents apiece, sawed or hand-hewn.

The mill we purchased was 10 miles north of old Fort Colville. It included a steam engine and boiler, all in good condition, and was rated to produce about 25,000 board feet of lumber per day.

The full price was $275. We paid $50 down, and had to cut railroad ties by hand and sell them to complete the payment before we could take posession of the mill.

It was larger than we wanted, but we could modify it for our purposes. For portability, we needed a smaller power plant. This is where the 6-cylinder gasoline engine from the old Studebaker hearse came into the picture.

We purchased the engine with the hearse attached for $25 from an auto dealer in Colville.

Our first problem was the transmission; it had been damaged and was locked in high gear.

To reach our destination we had to drive about 20 miles, all in high gear, over country roads.

We weren't even

We converted the two beautiful leather-upholstered seats into rocking chairs and used them as furniture.

sure we could climb some of the hills en route. One of us had to sit on the front fender and feed gas to the vacuum tank from a can to keep the engine running. However, we arrived home without any further mechanical trouble.

We operated the mill from 1934–1941 without any major problems from the Studebaker engine. In addition to railroad ties, we sawed lumber—fir, larch and pine—which we delivered locally for $11 per 1,000 board feet.

The body of the hearse had served its life and was abandoned—except for the two beautiful leather-upholstered seats.

We converted those into rocking chairs and used them as household furniture. The faithful old engine was finally junked and went into the wartime scrap-iron pile.

So ended the final chapter in the life of that Studebaker hearse. ❖

Paying for My First Car

By H.R. Plum

In October 1937 I got my first car, a 1928 two-door Model A. I bought it from the dealer in Elkton, Va. Not having money to pay for the car, I had to make a deal with him. He owned some wooded land, and he told me I could chop cordwood instead of paying cash. To complete the deal, I would have to chop 100 cords of wood.

I got in the car and drove to the top of the Blue Ridge Mountains to try it out. As I topped a mountain, I was doing 30 mph, so I figured I had a good car. When I returned to the dealership, I told him I'd take it. He filled it with gas at no extra charge and I drove it home.

I was a farmer, and I had corn to husk and gather in. I had to work at that every day until I got it all under cover. By the time the corn was all in, it was early November, so I took myself and three or four of my brothers to the mountains to chop wood.

Snow had already begun to fall in the mountains and in the valley, and most days we waded through knee-deep snow. To keep warm we burned brush, setting our frozen lunches on the coals to thaw.

On average, each of us cut two cords a day. Occasionally all of us together could cut a combined 10 cords in a day. A week before Christmas, two cousins from Hagerstown, Md., came to spend their Christmas vacation with us. They joined us to chop wood.

On Jan. 2, 1938, I went to the car dealer and picked up the title. As I did, he asked me how I managed to chop 100 cords so quickly. ❖

My Old Tin Ford

Author Unknown

Of my old tin Ford they all make fun;
They say she was born in 1901.
Well, maybe she was, but this I'll bet:
She's good for many a long mile yet!

The windshield's gone and the radiator leaks,
The fan belt slips and the horsepower squeaks,
She shakes the nuts and bolts all loose—
But she gets 40 miles on a gallon of juice.

When I can't get gas I use kerosene;
I've driven her home on paraffin!
There's a rattle in the front and a grind in the rear
And a Chinese puzzle for a steering gear.

The coils are dead and the plugs smoke fire,
The piston rings are baling wire,
But in spite of this, she's pulled me through,
And that's about all any car can do.

With high-priced cars they give you tools,
Some extra parts and a book of rules.
Wire stretchers and a pair of shears
Are all I've carried in 15 years.

But if I live to see the day
When she falls to pieces like the "One-Hoss Shay,"
If old Hank Ford stays in the game,
I'll buy another by the same old name.

Work & Prayer

By Angeline Kasl

"*Modli se a pracju*" ("Work and prayer") defined my Czechoslovakian parents' way of life.

One of my favorite memories is of watching my mother, Angela, making paper flowers for the graves of loved ones in November, a Catholic tradition. The roses she so patiently cut, curled and assembled were beautiful! Our deceased family members had the prettiest graves in the cemetery.

There was always a special bouquet for the graves of my Staricek and Starenka (great-grandmother and great-grandfather), perhaps because Mom couldn't put any on the graves of her own parents, who were buried in Texas.

Many times as a child, I'd look out to Mom's garden, and there she'd be, pulling weeds in her poppy seed patch. *What a picture! I remember thinking. My mother among the huge purple blooms waving in the breeze.*

> *When I got home after what seemed like the longest 1½ miles I had ever walked, I found Mom on her knees in the kitchen, praying.*

At harvesttime we cut the big poppy seed heads by the tubful and watched the seeds flow when the tops were cut off and the heads turned upside down. We would have a large tub of poppy seed to sell at 10 cents a pound. With this money we ordered fabric at 15 cents a yard from the Sears catalog, from which I chose the material for my school dresses.

In her spare time Mom also sewed for other people for extra money. In all her life she never bought a pattern. She just took a close look at the person she was sewing for. Seldom did she have to alter a garment.

She also "made over" old clothes into new ones. She saved every scrap of fabric for hand-pieced quilts. Mom also loved to crochet, and made everything from fancy doilies to rag rugs.

My dad, Emil, had hobbies, too, which earned extra money. One of his interests was beekeeping. In the spring we watched anxiously as the bees flew in and out of his rows of hives. Fresh clover honey on homemade bread—yum!

In the fall, Dad lifted the supers full of honeycomb and brought them inside to be processed in tubs over a slow fire in the kitchen range.

When cool, the wax would separate from the honey. My job was to have the jars washed and ready to be filled with the finished product. Jars covered the kitchen counters.

During the '30s our family was plagued by the grasshopper invasion, the Depression, drought and dust storms. One week the wind blew from the south for several days. I remember being at school when suddenly it became so dark that we couldn't read from our textbooks. The phone rang; a member of the board was calling school off. The teacher sent us home.

Walking home it was very still, and we could see only a few rods ahead of us. I'll never forget that awesome feeling. It made me think of the day when Christ died on the cross and darkness covered the earth. When I got home after what seemed like the longest 1½ miles I had ever walked, I found Mom on her knees in the kitchen, praying.

Dad was still out in the field drilling oats. We could hear his "Giddy-up!" and "Gee!" and "Haw!" and the creak of the harness and the occasional snort as if the horses were trying to clear the red dust from their throats. But even though they were only a few rods away, I couldn't see them. I will never forget that day as long as I live.

By the next morning it had cleared up a bit, but that fine red dust had settled over everything in the house.

During those hard times Mom always managed to have a few pennies left to buy embroidery floss so I could embroider. On hot summer afternoons we'd go down the cellar and sew. With the only light coming through the cellar door, I'd do needlepoint and Mom would piece quilts or patch everyday clothes. Sometimes as we stitched she sang to me or told me stories. She had fond memories of her childhood and recalled the many pranks her three brothers pulled.

Almost everyone had a cellar in those days, and they were dug by hand. Dad built ours 12 by 20 feet. I could see Dad's spade marks on the walls. The ceiling was railroad ties covered with packed dirt. One side of our cellar was lined with shelves of canned fruit and vegetables. In the fall, a stone jar of kraut stood in one corner and a bin of potatoes stood in another, and bright orange pumpkins were heaped nearby.

The cellar was also our storm cellar. Many times the family gathered there during the summer when a bad storm threatened. Dad always brought his rosary with him and would recite it in Czech by the light of a kerosene lamp. While the storm raged outside, we were safe and at peace.

Another memory of those days gone by is crawling under the perina (feather bed) with a warm flatiron at my feet on cold winter nights. Our upstairs bedrooms were always unheated. When we awoke early the next morning, there would be frost on top of the feather bed, and we'd hear Mom or Dad downstairs shaking the ashes down in the old cookstove, our only source of heat. Many times a layer of ice would have formed on the bucket of drinking water.

I also like to remember Dad's homemade forge where he shaped and sharpened his plowshares. I can still hear him hammering away at red-hot metal, and see him forming it into hinges and locks of all sizes. Sometimes he let me turn the fan to make the fire burn hotter.

Dad's favorite pastime was carving miniatures from wood. In the barn he had a small workshop where he spent Sunday afternoons, whittling away or sanding tiny figures. He sold them as fast as he made them.

He was good with a hammer and saw, too, building intricate squirrel cages. I cried when he sold one he had painted pink; I wanted it for Billy, my pet squirrel!

Yes, work and prayer were a way of life for my parents. Hard work kept our family of six clothed, fed and comfortable. But their faith in God helped them through all the heartbreaks and sacrifices as my parents lovingly cared for their children in hopes of a better tomorrow. ❖

Block Party!

By Beryl Yocum

Saturday Night Block Party!" the sign read, and I smiled. In this day and age it might mean rock music, guitar-playing, dancing in the street, refreshments. The placard was perched on the lawn of a sorority house near the University of Pennsylvania, so I could guess that it was an alfresco dance party for college students.

A flashback conjured up another type of block party—the kind I remembered from the years before World War I. In the old part of Philadelphia where I lived then, such parties were the highlight of the summer for me and my seven younger brothers and sisters.

Having a big family never kept Mama from doing her bit for needy poor children. Aided by neighbors and under the sponsorship of the old *North American*, a daily newspaper, Mama took on the stint year after year. The newspaper furnished publicity, decorations and enough bricks of tricolored Neopolitan ice cream to insure the affair's success.

Business was good, and we all worked like beavers until the last slice of cake, the last melting drop of ice cream were sold. Then the "help" went on a long hayride.

Fate was usually kind weatherwise, and on the big night the porches on 44th Street glowed with the romantic light of Japanese lanterns. They were also strung along the sidewalks from tree to tree. Miraculously, they never caught fire, though today they'd be considered a fire hazard.

Booths dotted the pavement at strategic spots, offering cakes, candies, fancy goods and lemonade. Dishes of ice cream and slices of cake were served at trestle tables in someone's large front yard, and Victrola music added to the gala atmosphere. To the youngsters' great delight, there was a fish pond, a fortune teller and a hayride, and all were well patronized.

For a nickel kids could cast a rod over a three-ply green burlap screen and come up with a wonderfully wrapped package. It was someone's "white elephant," but to the buyer, it was a treasure from the Indies—Japanese water flowers, silk and paper fans, a hoop to roll, a storybook, anything that would keep a youngster busy for a few hours during the long, hot summer.

Girls from age 12 on were considered young ladies, and booths were manned by an adult and two of these young ladies. Sales ladies wore white organdy and pompadours with hair bows big enough to take them airborne. My sweet tooth tied me to the candy booth where I helped dispense the grainy fudge in all shades of chocolate, divinity, cream mints, cinnamon Irish potatoes and jaw-breakers—molasses taffy that lasted for hours.

A baker of no mean note herself, Mother always presided at the cake booth, and passersby admired and bought cupcakes, drop cakes, Lady Baltimore cakes and melt-in-the-mouth pies—items that sometimes went for the astronomical price of 75 cents! Kids could wangle a giant cookie for a penny and wash it down with lemonade for 3 cents a glass.

Weeks of work by many ladies went into the fancywork booth, and I still recall a blue satin fan-shaped needle book I bought there and used for years. There were hand-painted china items, pin trays, match receivers, ink stands, shaving mugs, and silk slipper bags in which one carried dancing slippers to dancing school and parties, as well as aprons, dust caps and handmade linen hankies—great for early Christmas gifts.

The good, sweet smell of hay filled a horse-drawn truck driven by a serious older man from the livery stable. Need I add that a chaperone accompanied each hitch of the ride, which covered a distance of 10 blocks or so. It cost kids a nickel, and adults a dime. Glee-club singing made the rides fly by quickly, and often older teen-age girls got their first kiss on that hayride.

The fortune teller's booth was contrived by heavy drapes hung over a clothesline, and it was so dark we could never identify the seer. Our spines tingled. After we crossed her palm with silver, she told all. Tall dark strangers, unex-

pected windfalls, lucky surprises, a long trip—these were among the lucky things predicted. Never was there a hint of evil or misfortune, and to this day I am a pushover for anyone who even hints of foretelling the future.

Business was always good, and we all worked like beavers until the last slice of cake, the last melting drop of ice cream were sold. Then all the "help" went on a long hayride.

My mother, God bless her, usually wound up with a princely sum such as $63 to turn over to the Fresh Air Fund. The real reward, though, came a few days later when we scanned the Sunday issue of the *North American*. There, in a fuzzy group picture, we basked in our first taste of real newspaper publicity: "and of the young people on North 44th Street, reading from left to right—" ❖

Relative Riches

By Clara Comstock

*W*ay back when, every farm family—and even those in small towns—had a cow and some chickens. Besides providing food, they brought in a little cash "pin money." I doubt that we ever bought chicken feed. Our chickens ate out by the barn and ranged out into the woods. Sometimes a coyote got one.

Everyone had a few guineas, too; they made good "watchdogs." They roosted in the trees, and if we heard them squawk in the night, we knew we'd better load up the shotgun and go see what was wrong. Perhaps it was an owl looking for a meal, or a possum getting too close, or even a two-legged varmint prowling 'round the henhouse.

Guineas were good eating, too; they tasted something like wild game. They hustled food for themselves, too, ranging miles from home, but they could fly better than the chickens and so were seldom caught by a coyote or wolf. It was a common sight—a bunch of guineas lined up on a fence, all calling, "Pot-rack, pot-rack, pot-rack!"

I can't remember many rich people; neither can I recall anyone who was really destitute. Some made more than others, and some were better managers.

Chickens were very important. Everyone hatched their own and most were mixed breeds. But sometimes someone might get a setting of special eggs. There was always a speckled little banty hen (everyone kept a few bantams as they laid well and were good little mothers) with baby chicks. Perhaps one of us kids had even found a few quail eggs and slipped them under her. I doubt that the baby quail understood their "biddy hen" mother, but they stayed with her until they were half-grown. Then "the call of the wild" urged them to forsake their bantam foster mother.

We ate lots of frying chickens in the summer and fall, and baking hens in the winter, with dressing and dumplin's. Chicken soup was the first food given to a sick person.

Chickens were good to sell, too. They could always be counted on to bring in a few extra dollars in an emergency.

The family milk cow was a pet and was treated very specially. We always had a little Jersey who was milked at a regular hour and milked clean each time. Mama did the milking. She didn't trust anyone else to do it properly; if it wasn't done right, the cow would "go dry."

Sometimes a boy would drive our cow along with several of the neighbors' cows out to a good range for the day. Our cow wore a bell so we could always find her. If, one day, she did manage to hide out where we couldn't find her, we could count on her to come in sometime during the night with a little, long-legged calf at her side.

Every family had a place to keep their butter and milk cool—perhaps a natural spring, where the crocks and buckets could be set in the cool, shallow water. Or, it might be hung down inside the well. But if milk spilled into the well, the well would have to be drained so clear water could run in.

We had a milk vat by the well. It was a large wooden box with a heavy lid and a "runoff hole" just below the tops of the milk containers. Every time we drew a bucket of water for the house, we drew an extra one to pour into the milk vat to keep the milk surrounded by fresh, cold water.

We sent our eggs and butter to town and sold them, but we never sold buttermilk or sweet milk. If the cow ran dry, a neighbor would share some of his milk. It was the same with garden stuff; if one person had too much, he gave it to someone else, and he, in return, might have a surplus of something else to share. One of our customs was that if someone borrowed a dish (or a basket, or a bucket), she never returned it empty.

I can't remember many rich people, but neither can I recall anyone who was really destitute. Some made more than others, and some were better managers.

I remember one family; the man of the house cut wood for a living, but wood was selling for just $1 a rick and they didn't seem to be managing very well. Their daughter Vernie was just younger than I. Since I only had

younger brothers, my own clothes couldn't be handed down. So, each fall, Mama would put my outgrown clothes in a sack. Then we'd go visit the woodcutter's family.

Now, we didn't just go in and say, "Here's some old clothes for your kids." We'd sit and visit awhile. We kids would go out and swing or "see-saw" on a board across a sawhorse. Finally, Mama would say we had to go, and she'd add, "Oh, I brought some of Clara's dresses she's outgrown. Maybe Vernie can play in them

to save her good school dresses." (My old ones were better than Vernie's Sunday best.)

They'd lay the clothes out on the bed and say yes, they'd about fit, and she could play in them. Then the woman would go get something to give to us.

As we walked the mile home, each of carrying a half-gallon of unsweetened blackberries, I asked Mama why in the world we took them, as we had blackberries all over the place. She explained it would hurt her feelings if she didn't give us something in return. The next "burn out" we heard of, we sent the blackberries with enough sugar to sweeten them.

The Golden Rule was taken very seriously in those days, and it worked out very well. ❖

Making Our Own Fun

Memories of making our own fun when there was no budget for it always take us back to tougher—but somehow better—days.

One of my favorite memories is from a summer day way back when.

The August sun seared its way into our lives again that morning long ago. Another day without rain. Oh, well, the crops were long since burned to a crisp in the brutal drought. Summer refused to give in to the steadily shortening days and the relentless onslaught of the season.

It was a brutal afternoon for a boy of 12. The breeze—even on the hilltop we called home—refused to blow. The creeks had been reduced to a few tepid waterholes barely able to accommodate hot tired feet. Even the shade of the huge oaks surrounding my home refused to give much comfort; the leaves seemed to be losing their lock on life already—two months before they should. My pal Chester walked up through the heat, carrying his rifle and suggesting an afternoon squirrel hunt.

"Aw, it's too hot to hunt," I said. "Probably wouldn't see anything anyway."

"C'mon," Chet retorted, "I didn't walk 2 miles just to sit here and sweat. Besides, I know a place we can cool off."

That hope was enough to pull me away from the front yard and elicit permission from Mama. With my single-shot .22 under my arm I jawed at Chet as I reached the edge of the yard: "Well, what's keepin' ya?"

Chet was quickly in the lead. Over a couple of hills—and the dells between—we plodded. I had been right; neither rabbit nor squirrel rousted about in the August heat. The only sound was the chirp of the cicada and the soft padding of our feet, wary for prey. Instead of directing us toward the third rise, Chet turned parallel to the slope and headed toward an outcropping of rocks. I knew of a cave spring which normally flowed from the base of these rocks; I also knew the water long since had subsided with the drought of the summer, sinking to subterranean rocks.

"I found it last week," Chet said as we neared the cave. A farmer had dug out the mouth of the cave and had run piping back to what must have been a small reservoir. He had built a sizable holding box for the precious water; lowing of nearby cattle told me his work had not been in vain.

At first we dipped handfuls of the pure, cold spring water, then wetted handkerchiefs for faces and hot, dirty necks.

At first we dipped handfuls of the pure, cold spring water, then wetted handkerchiefs for faces and hot, dirty necks. Next we were sitting on the edge of the box, feet dangling frigidly inside as we talked. Dare led to double-dare and soon we were in the spring box—where we stayed until the icy water forced us out.

By the time we walked home, it was evening. I guess our body temperatures had dropped enough not to notice the heat. That night the breeze still wouldn't blow and the house was just as hot.

Yet, without a penny to spend, Chet and I had had more fun than princes could tell of. I don't think I've spent a more simply joyful summer's afternoon in all the decades since.

Chet has been dead for quite a few years now. Janice and I never have air-conditioned the old farmhouse, so those August afternoons sometimes remind me of that brutally hot day from my youth long ago. What I wouldn't give to see Chet walk up, rifle in hand, ready to search out another deliciously cool spring box. There are some things that money just can't buy. Making our own fun taught us that back in the Good Old Days.

—Ken Tate, Editor

Fun in the Good Old Days

By Edna P. Bates

Most entertainment was do-it-yourself during Depression times when I was young. No radio or TV filled hours each day. As a matter of fact, we had few spare hours to fill. Helping on the farm took most of our summer holidays and some of the few winter hours left after homework was done. There were always eggs to be gathered, wiped, graded and candled. That was a girl's job, but so was driving horses to spray fruit trees

or bring in the hay, gathering up stones in the fields each spring, and picking fruit all summer. There were three girls in our family; no boys.

Movies had no place in our young lives. We were 10 miles from the city and had no money for such luxuries anyway. I was well into my teens when I saw my first film, *As You Desire Me* with Greta Garbo.

There were no Little League baseball, football or hockey teams, and no Brownies, Guides or Scouts in our neighborhood. In fact, grown-ups felt no obligation at all to entertain us!

If we had completed all our chores, we were happy to grab a book and head for the big tree on the lawn where my sister had improvised a hammock by fastening a strip of rag carpet with some nails. The elm's boughs hung right to the ground like a big umbrella. Once we were up in it, no one could see us. "Out of sight, out of mind" was our idea!

But don't waste any sympathy on our "deprived" youth! We were certainly poor, but I wish today's young people could be as "underprivileged" as we were! We had lots of fun, most of which we made ourselves.

On Saturday evenings in the winter, neighbors often dropped in, or we went to visit them. Our parents talked while we kids played games. We popped corn and ate apples—both grown on the farm. We often gathered around the piano while my mother played and had a sing-song.

Once or twice each winter someone would host a progressive Crokinole party. We practiced at home many evenings, hoping to play well enough to win a prize at these parties. My dad was a crack shot with a true eye and steady hand. I never did beat him! Each lady brought whatever she made best for the bountiful lunch that was served when the games were over.

During winter, the Literary Society met once a month. Perhaps much that went on there had rather dubious literary value, but everyone enjoyed it. We were sure that our own Jimmy P. could have given Harry Lauder a run for his

On Saturday evenings in the winter, neighbors often dropped in, or we went to visit them. Our parents talked while we kids played games.

money when he pinned a plaid rug around himself for a kilt and, with the help of a crooked stick, pranced bare-legged around the stage, his Scottish accent lending a genuine touch to *I Belong to Glasgow* or (to my shy sister Carrie's intense embarrassment) *I'm Going to Marry-arry Sweet Little Carrie-arrie*!

Many young people had their first taste of practice on the platform at the old "Lit." In fact, I made my first speech in a public-speaking contest there. I spoke learnedly about "Chicken Raising," a topic which—however dull—I did know about. (I'd begun early, as a "lantern carrier" for my dad, when he dosed the unsuspecting hens with "roup cure" as they slept on their perches. That's the only time you can catch a hen!) I still cherish the leather-bound copy of *Black Beauty* which I won as fourth prize. I read it and reread it and cried over it.

As a teen, I debated for the first time at the same Literary Society. My partner was a youngish bachelor whom I knew only by sight. He came to our house one evening to prepare the points with which we hoped to demolish our "worthy opponents'" arguments. I forget what the topic was, but I do remember two things: He had eaten onions for supper (which did not add to his charm), and we lost! The experience was good for us, though. Today I can give a prepared speech and answer questions "off the cuff" without getting nervous.

We put on plays, too. My first role was that of the pathetic little black orphan slave, Topsy, in *Uncle Tom's Cabin*. I still remember some of my lines. I sobbed bitterly when my little mistress, the angelic Eva, went to join the angels.

We put on this play at half a dozen community halls besides our own. We were always fed afterward, but my pride kept me from getting much lunch. By the time I got all the burnt cork off my face, the rest of the cast had eaten up the food. "Uncle Tom" always recovered miraculously from his beating at the hands of

Simon Legree, and ate with his blackface still on, more interested in food than pride! I owe all my success to my playing acting, all dressed up in front of the old oval mirror in the attic.

Scarcity of money didn't stop us from having parties. Our big living room didn't have furniture so good that we couldn't have fun there! Many of our party games were pretty rambunctious.

One popular game was Wink, in which the boys stood behind the chairs with a girl in front of them. One boy with an empty chair would wink at a girl. She would try to slip out of her chair before the boy behind her could grab her. (It was against the rules to touch until after someone winked.)

Then the places were reversed so that the girls could wink at their favorite guys. (Shades of "women's liberation," decades ahead of its time!)

How well I remember my disgrace when I grabbed a boy to prevent his escape, caught my hand in his pocket, and ripped his brand-new jacket!

Fruit Basket was another strenuous game we liked. Of course, Spin the Bottle and Post Office—the "kissing games"—turned up at most parties. Cross Questions and Silly Answers and Consequences made for a rest between rougher games as they were pencil-and-paper games in which we wrote things down and read out the ludicrous combinations.

My Grandfather's Old Green Britches and Poor Pussy tested our ability to keep a straight face while everyone else tried to make us laugh. Charades were fun, too. I never could decide which I enjoyed more—acting out the syllables

of our word, or trying to figure what word the others were trying to illustrate.

One young fellow was a master at telling ghost stories. I remember sitting in the dark on our veranda one summer night, frozen with horror, as we listened to his bloodcurdling tales of bloodstained hands and headless horsemen!

Lunch wasn't expensive, but it was delicious and filling: sandwiches made with my mother's good homemade bread and butter, my father's home-cured ham, egg salad from the family hens, layer cakes, doughnuts and raspberry tarts made with lard rendered from our own pork and raspberries from our own patch, preserved in summer. Mom's coffee with thick cream from our own cows was always good.

My parents didn't go out for the evening when we had a party, as kids nowadays seem to expect. In fact, everyone would have been surprised if they had—and disappointed, too. They enjoyed our parties, and our friends liked having them there.

My dad was quite a cutup. One night we had a taffy pull. Mom made the taffy and poured it onto greased plates to cool. Then we girls greased our hands and pulled it until it was firm and almost white. Finally we cut it off in chunks to eat.

My dad put a bit of water on one girl's piece when he handed it to her, and of course it stuck to her hands like glue. For a long while she couldn't figure out why her taffy was different from the rest! He'd picked someone with a good sense of humor, of course.

We didn't forget that if you really want to have fun, you can't buy it. No store can deliver it. You just go ahead and do it yourself! ❖

CHARLES
BERGER

Fun When We Were Young

By Mary Peak

Most children can entertain themselves. I hear the little girls next door recite their rhythmic singsong as they jump rope. It takes me back to my children's school years and to my own youth. Now I can hardly believe I ever jumped "hot pepper"! I loved to swing. We all did, and we fussed over turns. Dad made a swing wide enough for all three of us. He said he didn't want to hear any more fussing. Bet we did, though. I used to dream of swinging real high and I'd hit the bed with a bounce when I fell. My sister would scold when I did.

We played all the usual outdoor games—cowboys and Indians, hide and seek, wood tag, and run-sheepy-run. Did you ever chew up shee-shower to see who could make the worst face, or play statues?

On bad days we gathered around the dining table for jackstraws, tiddly winks, Authors, dominoes, or a rousing game of Pit. Later we played carroms with the board and taws. When we had company, Mama sometimes said she would cut a piece of pie for all the winners, but we were all winners.

> *On bad days we gathered around the dining table for jackstraws, tiddly winks, Authors, dominoes, or a rousing game of Pit.*

One summer, one of the boys in the neighborhood had broken a leg at a track meet; we played a lot of carrom that summer. At night all of us—at least all but that one boy—played run-sheepy-run under the streetlight and for blocks around.

In winter when we were small, Mama sometimes got out her zither and the delicate music written in German. We watched closely as she tuned the zither. Sometimes she had my older sister sound a note on the piano. Pick in hand, she ran over the chords. Then she was ready to play the *Valse*, our favorite. It had several runs which used most of the strings. Mama said she had once played in an orchestra made up of zithers of all sizes. A German man led with an "Ein, zwei, drei!" I would have loved to have heard that orchestra!

Sometimes Mama used toothpicks and corks of different sizes to make dancers for the sounding board of the zither. When she played a fast

number, they really danced around!

When we got too old for dolls we played with paper dolls. Most of the time we made our own dolls and doll clothes. Wallpaper was the "fabric" for most of the clothing. If we had colored tissue paper, we used it to make ball gowns. When I moved recently, I found some of those old dolls and their dresses in a stationery box. I haven't seen a child play with paper dolls in years!

We dressed up and played house all the time. My cousin and I used the top of the cave as a stage and put on programs.

Boys were the original recyclers. They made wagons and scooters. When someone threw away a baby buggy, they were in business, and built something using the wheels. A broken skate and some boards made a scooter.

They whittled tops and played marbles and mumblety-peg. Every time an inner tube on the car went bad, they soon had a slingshot made. Whenever some old boards surfaced with no use for them, they made stilts. When the weeds dried in the fall, they used the hollow stems for bean shooters. In summer, they smoked cornsilk or grapevine.

My sister and I took piano lessons, and later my brother did, as well. At my first recital I got lost playing *Happy Farmer*, much to everyone's embarrassment. My parents decided lessons were a waste of time for me. Musically speaking, when I went to the well I had a leaky bucket.

At high-school age we played tennis with a group of young people. In the group was the minister's son, who had a fine voice. When he left our town, he went into a large city to sing with

continued on next page

Homemade Toys of the '30s

By Lettie L. Wood

Remember the homemade toys of the 1930s? My brother, sister and I made most of ours during those tough Depression years. Money was unheard of, but we were blessed with parents who taught us to make do. Here are a few of our homemade toys with brief and simple directions on how to make them.

Wooden Stilts

We not only made these—we actually walked on them without ever getting any broken bones! Wooden stilts were made from two 2-by-4s and a thick wedge from a hand-length split block. The 2-by-4s were cut the same length as the child's height. A wedge-shaped block was then nailed onto each 2-by-4, about 12 inches from the bottom. Holding the top of a stilt in each hand and placing each foot on a wedge-block, the child walked around stiff-legged in a world of his own.

Tin-Can "Tom Walkers"

For each tom walker (you'll need two), turn an empty 16-ounce (or larger) can upside down with the open end on the bottom. Punch two holes, one across from the other, just below the top end (closed end).

Bend a long piece of wire into a U-shape and insert an end through each hole, from outside of can into inside. Check wire for length: the curved end, which is the handhold, should reach the child's fingertips as he stands with arms hanging at his sides so he can comfortably hold this "handle."

Secure the wire handle at its proper length by winding the loose ends together tightly inside the can; using the "handle," pull wires inside can and snugly against bottom of can lid.

Insert a foot between wires on closed end of can; use handles to hold cans snugly against the bottoms of your feet as you walk about.

Slingshot

One Y-shaped tree limb is cut to fit easily in the hand for the stock. You will also need two ½- by 8-inch rubber bands from an old inner tube, one old shoe tongue and twine.

Make a notch around the end of each of the Y-forks. Tie on bands at notch. Make holes on each end of the shoe tongue. Attach heavy twine in holes at end of tongue pocket. Tie other ends to rubber bands. ❖

continued from previous page

a choir and a large band. The people who ran the telephone exchange had a crystal radio set, the first in our town. They invited our group to come and hear Jim sing on the radio. We had to take turns—there was only a single set of earphones—but we did hear him sing. When he finished the concert with *Pistol-Packin' Mama*, we knew he was thinking of us, as that had been our song.

In card games, we played pitch and pinochle. They were a lot of fun. When I was a schoolteacher we played bridge at our parties.

Seems to me children today are smarter than we were. There is a world of bright books to read. They have paint-by-number sets and puzzles of all kinds. They even work crossword puzzles! When a half-pint sails through a crossword puzzle I had trouble with, it gets my dander up.

But still, we didn't have to look for something to keep us busy. Perhaps television is taking away children's ability for creative playing. Back then creativity was about all we had a lot of. Life was hard sometimes, but at least we had fun along the way. ❖

Old Philadelphia Street Games

By Richard P. Borkowski

After hearing what it cost a boy to play baseball today, my mind shifted back to a well-worn cobblestone street along the Delaware River in Philadelphia, back to when we played all kinds of sports and games all day long (and most of the evening, if the street lamps worked), without costing us or our parents a single penny.

A worn-out broom was quickly converted into a baseball bat. A 3-inch piece of rubber garden hose served as a baseball. A small rolled-up notebook was an official street football.

Anytime a game called for a real ball, someone would plead with the janitor of a nearby warehouse to "see if there are any old balls on the roof." Somehow, there always was. That roof was our own athletic equipment center.

I never realized it then, but we surely saved our parents a lot of money. Take, for example, the savings in travel expense. We never had to travel from one field to another. The widest, least-traveled street with a lot of natural boundaries (like curbs, lampposts and trees) was our baseball diamond, our basketball court, and our football field. If we needed a home plate, someone found a brick or loose cobblestone. Bases ranged from broken curbs to ice wagons. The gutters served as our football sidelines, and any unusually marked area on a wall was our basketball hoop.

> *Bases ranged from curbs to ice wagons. Gutters served as football sidelines, and any unusually marked area on a wall was our basketball hoop.*

The greatest savings to our parents was in the area of coaches and umpires. Who needed a guy with a master's degree to teach us games for $10,000 a year? We had our own list of official games to fit any terrain and situation—like the day one of those troublesome automobiles broke down around second base. We formed a quick huddle, and the car became second base for that day.

Our means of deciding any close play was perfect. The biggest guy in any game made all questionable calls, and the game played on. I wonder if the nine officials in today's pro football system are an improvement over our system.

Each of our street games was full of traditions and customs. One never broke the unwritten policies of game selection. "Hey, how about halfball today?" someone would shout.

"No, sir—let's play hoseball!"

"We played that yesterday! Today it's stickball!"

After everyone had mentioned a dozen games apiece we'd pause and look to the biggest guy.

"Today," he would announce, "we will start off with hoseball!"

Naturally, the guy who owned the equipment had a say in which game we chose, especially if he threatened to take his stuff home or to another street.

The next order of business was to choose up sides. The best two players flipped anything that had one side you could call "heads" and another "tails." Sometimes it was even a coin. The winner was permitted first choice. Pitching a stone to see who was closest to a line and shooting out fingers to win your choice of odd or even were other means of drafting teams.

My favorite way of choosing up was tossing a stick. Each captain attempted to place his hand at the top by alternating grasps with his opponent after one tossed the stick at the other.

What a contest of strategy and hand-squeezing to get your hand to the top of the stick! Who-ever succeeded then had to twirl it around his head three times without dropping it. Next he held it out at arm's length while the other tried to kick it out of his hand.

If he survived all that, he got first choice.

The ground rules also had to be discussed.

"A hit past the lamp post is a single. Anything past the car is a double. Jack's step is a triple; anything past the corner on a fly is a homer."

The only unbreakable, almost holy rule on our street concerned the games we could and could not play during certain times of the year.

Spring and summer meant baseball only. Fall was football, and winter meant either basketball or hockey. Of course, we seldom played the official versions of these games, and no one really knew when one season "officially" ended and the other began. It always worked out though. It had something to do with the biggest guy again.

Baseball on the Philadelphia streets really meant hoseball, or Philadelphia stickball, or mushball, or halfball. Sometimes we'd play hoseball for a month straight. Another time we'd play the entire series of summer games in a single day.

Hoseball was my game. Cut the broom off the broomstick for a bat. Find an old garden hose and cut it into 3-inch pieces for balls. (Our neighborhood always seemed to have short water hoses.)

The rules were close to those for baseball except that you didn't have to run after hitting the ball. That's what I liked about hoseball. If you hit it a certain distance and it wasn't caught, it was a single, a double or whatever.

The only people who didn't like hoseball were the people who owned windows.

Philly stickball was the most popular because it was the closest to baseball and it made everyone feel rich—we had to use a real ball. A broomstick, a ball, four bricks for bases, and it was play ball all day—or until the ball broke.

I've since tried to establish the difference between Philly stickball and the New York variety. So far the only difference I've been able to find seems to be that one was played on Philadelphia streets and the other was played on the streets of New York.

The hardest part of my childhood was trying to hit a knuckleball-curve-spitter applied to a dead ball with a broomstick.

Philly stickball was the most popular because it was the closest to baseball.

Mushball was always played after stickball. When the ball was really, really dead and starting to rip, we'd stuff it with old rags and paper and wrap it with some black tape. Stickball now became mushball.

When the mushball started to break, it was time for the game every pitcher loved: halfball. The Wright brothers must have pitched halfball prior to their great discovery.

Halfball was just like hoseball, except that half of a ball was pitched. This half moon was the remains of a mushball, which had once been a stickball. A halfball pitched underhand looks like a soft, miniature Frisbee flipping and flopping to the whim of every air current. It can drop 5 feet over the plate, or rise two stories.

In the fall, the game was football. To be specific, it was assignment-book football. Who could afford a real football?! It seems that long ago in the folklore of our neighborhood, a boy wanted to play football so badly that he made the supreme sacrifice by rolling up his small school assignment book. A rubber band was wrapped around it and assignment-book football was born.

The game is like touch football without a football. Oh, those long pass patterns down the curb! A fake at the ice wagon, in and out of the vacant lot, a great one-hand catch—and six points! What hidden-ball tricks, corner-to-

corner passes, and what arguments about whether he tagged him with one hand or two! The height of skill was required to punt the 4-inch assignment book on fourth down.

When winter arrived the street became a hockey and basketball arena. If it snowed we played tin-can hockey for about a week straight, after clearing the snow. Another time it was our version of basketball we called ledgeball.

Tin-can hockey was played with or without sticks, and with or without a tin can. If a can couldn't be found, we substituted a rock, a halfball or someone's sneak. (It was never the biggest guy's sneak.) Nevertheless, the game was still called tin-can hockey.

Ledgeball basketball became part of our street schedule when Fatty Plotski discovered the "ledge"—a small overhang above the warehouse garage doors. If you could shoot the basketball (normally a 3-inch bouncy ball found on the roof) so that it struck the top side of the ledge, that was a field goal. Foul shots were only given in cases of blood. Ever try to dribble a 3-inch ball on cobblestones, up a curb, shoot at a foot-long ledge, and try to avoid meeting a garage door? Ledgeball was never a polished game, but it was exciting.

There were many other minor-league street games, like buck-buck, box ball, sidewalk tennis, bottle-top golf and blood alley, but they were played when a mother kicked us out of the street, or when the milkman's horse couldn't wait until the next street.

Today most city streets are too clogged, too dirty and too unsafe for a return to these games. Our tremendous love for games has somehow been detoured to commercialism. Game rules for kids are engraved carefully in official booklets for all neighborhoods, cities and countries. A tin can seldom replaces an official hockey puck today.

Nevertheless, I'll always remember those simple, cheap, fun games on "our" street, especially when I pass a sporting goods store. Wonder if those stores would even be interested in handling old broomsticks? ❖

Work & Fun In the Hills

By Gladys Dinsmore Wright

Most of the people who lived in the hills of southwestern Virginia during the early 1900s were poor and uneducated, and had to fight the elements to survive. Most couples had eight or 10 children, and the rocky land produced barely enough food for their large families. If the mother lived to be 45, she looked 75.

My mother died three weeks after she gave birth to her ninth child. At age 40, she was worn out from child-bearing and hard work.

We lived up Devil's Wrath Path, between Natural Tunnel and Duffield, in Scott County. We lived mostly on the vegetables we raised in the garden. Most families had a cow and a hog or two. The hogs provided seasoning meat for our vegetables and lard for the biscuits. The cows gave us milk and butter.

We also took advantage of the wild game when it was in season—squirrels, opossums, rabbits, groundhogs and quail. These wild meats had to be soaked overnight in vinegar or buttermilk and cooked in a special way to be tasty.

Most families had a few chickens; we took the eggs to the store and exchanged them for flour, meal, sugar, coffee and fabric. We made all our clothes at home, using the old treadle sewing machine. We had one pair of shoes a year, ordered from a Sears and Roebuck catalog. If the shoes fit, fine; if they didn't, we wore them anyway. I have had blisters all over my feet from ill-fitting shoes.

When the soles wore thin, my daddy got out the old shoe last and put half-soles on them. We started going barefoot sometime in March or early April.

We had lots of fun in the good old days, but I'm afraid that today's generation would think our fun was nothing but work. We combined work and fun.

We had lots of fun in the good old days, but I'm afraid that today's generation would think our fun was nothing but work. But we combined work and fun.

In the fall, we made molasses. Some of the farmers grew sorghum cane, and when the stalks were ripe and juicy, we gathered to boil down the juice from the stalks until it was a thick syrup—sorghum molasses.

We called these events "stir-offs."

The cane mill had two stone rollers on a wooden contraption. A horse was hitched to the end of a long, wooden pole connected to the cane mill, and as the horse walked around in a circle, the rollers moved 'round and 'round. A man fed the cane stalks in between the rollers and the juice poured out into a big washtub on the other side. A clean grass bag covered the tub to catch the chaff and bugs.

The older folks did the work while the younger ones had a good time playing games and listening to the fiddlers, guitar players and banjo pickers who usually attended these events.

The menfolk kept the fire going under the homemade furnace and the women skimmed the green foam and bugs from the boiling sorghum juice.

When the apples were ripe, we had apple peelings at neighboring homes. While they worked, the neighbors hashed over all the gossip and had a good time, visiting as they worked.

When the juice had boiled down to a syrupy consistency, the resulting sorghum molasses was strained into 25- and 50-pound lard cans. Each person got a joint from a cane stalk and used it to eat out of the pans while they were being strained. Some folks brought pint buckets so they could take home enough molasses for their biscuits the next morning. In the hills, we used molasses to sweeten most of our homemade cakes, pies and fruits, and we ate it on our flapjacks as well as homemade biscuits.

When the apples were ripe, we had apple peelings at neighboring homes. The nearest neighbors came with their paring knives and peeled, cored and sliced the apples. While they worked, they hashed over all the gossip and had a good time, visiting as they worked.

The next day they cooked the apple slices into apple butter, cooking it in big brass pots over fires out in the yard. The apples had to be cooked slowly and stirred with a big, long, wooden stirrer to keep them from sticking. When the apples had cooked to mush and had turned a brownish color, it was time to add the sugar and cinnamon.

We stored the finished apple butter in gallon crocks in a dark, cool place where it lasted the year through. Apple butter was very good on hot biscuits, and on the cold biscuits we took to school for lunch.

When the wild strawberries and other berries were in season, the whole family went berry picking. We moved freely from hill to hill; no one minded whose land you were on. We canned the berries and made jams, jellies and preserves to enjoy during the long, cold winter.

We knew that anything we couldn't put up in the summertime, we would have to do without until the next time around.

Snakes were plentiful in the hills, but I guess God was looking after us. In the course of picking berries, we would go into undergrowth where we couldn't see what we were stepping on. None of our family was ever bitten by a snake in all our berry-picking years.

In the fall we gathered hickory nuts and walnuts. When the hulls were dry, we removed them and cracked the nuts on an old flatiron with a hammer. We sold the nutmeats to the country store and used the money to order Christmas presents for the family. Our presents were usually items of clothing that we needed. None of the country stores in the hills stocked toys, as most folks were too poor to buy them.

Corn-shucking parties were lots of fun! Courting couples attended these events with their parents. If a boy found an ear of corn with some blue grains, he got to kiss his girl. If he found blue and red grains, he got to hug and kiss her. If a couple found a solid red ear of corn, they could hug and kiss anytime they wanted during the shucking.

The older folks told ghost stories, and as most of the hill people were superstitious, most everyone was scared to go home.

As young children we had fun making rag dolls and doll clothes. No one I knew had store-bought dolls. When a doll got real dirty, we had

John Slobodnik

a big funeral for it. We sang hymns, said short prayers, and even read some from the Bible. After we put the doll in the grave we covered it with wildflowers. Sometimes we dug them up if our supply of dolls was running short.

We made moss dollhouses, with all the furniture made of moss, and the dolls crafted from sticks. Bed covers were leaves pinned together with thorns. We children had a lot of fun, and it didn't cost a dime.

Boys played with their jackknives, rolled wheels with a wire, and made flutter-mills out of tin cans in every stream. They built dams and enjoyed watching the water turn those old split cans 'round and 'round.

Each summer there was at least one big ice cream social. Families gathered at one of the country churches; ice was brought from a nearby town. Fresh cream, natural flavorings and a lot of cranking made some of the best dessert I've ever tasted.

Most everyone went to Sunday school and church on Sunday. The only people who didn't go were those who were so poor that they had no clothes to wear, or those who had a terrible sickness in the family. Most courting was done by the young couples as they went to and from church. All courting couples were chaperoned by their parents at all times. The parents walked about 10 feet behind or in front of the couple. It was mighty hard to steal a kiss with such strict parents!

Those may have been the good old days, and I do have many pleasant memories, but I am glad that my father was wise enough to send me away to boarding school to get an education. There I saw my first indoor bathroom, electricity, refrigerator and radio.

I learned that if one had an education, there was an easier and better way of life than the bare existence I had known. But although I have been out of the hills for 60 years, I shall never forget my roots. ❖

The Salt Baby

By Ruth Schenley

When I was a little tad—oh, 1916–1920, give or take a little—I played with a series of salt babies. They were most satisfactory companions.

What is a salt baby? Well, you can't get them today, except perhaps in a fake old-fashioned grocery store that deals in reproductions at outrageous prices, like penny candy for a quarter; but back then, the salt baby came to the house regularly with the grocery order. A salt baby was a cloth sack of table salt—in 5- and 10-pound sizes, a foot to 18 inches long, and 5 to 8 inches wide.

There was something about salt babies that was better than dolls. It was the thick, comfortable feel of them, the realistically flexible way they fitted the curve of a child's arm, and the fact that they seemed to absorb and return your warmth as you cuddled them. A doll feels artificial. A salt baby felt like a real baby.

When the salt baby arrived, I would seize it with glad cries and prance around, holding it like a live infant. Mama helped me wrap my salt babies in blankets and make them into personalized playmates. Sometimes we would tie a string about 4 inches from the top to form the head.

We would put my old baby cap on it and a baby dress on the rest. Mama used to draw a face on the salt baby's head by lightly inking in blue eyes and a red mouth.

Legs didn't matter—baby dresses were extra-long in those days—but we sometimes stuffed the arms with rags.

There was always a salt baby around. My parents kept supplies of staples ahead, and country folks used lots of salt in lots of ways. Mama was delighted with the salt baby idea and was careful to see that a new one had arrived before the old one had to be opened.

Playing with the salt baby didn't damage the contents at all. A well-dressed salt baby never got dingy. The contents always came out crystal white and pure when the sack was finally opened. Then, when the salt was used up, the bag joined the shelf of empty sugar and flour sacks which conscientious housewives of Mama's generation saved for various projects.

Sometimes I named the homemade toy, but mostly it was just called "Salt Baby."

There was something about salt babies that was better than dolls.

I was not the only one who crooned lullabies over salt babies in a little rocking chair and took them to bed at night. Other little girls around my age were doing the same thing in the homes of our relatives and friends.

The salt baby mystique was quite a thing in our neighborhood. I have dim memories of my cousins trying to make salt babies sit up in chairs at dolly tea parties, and I definitely recall how several of us wheeled them around in our outgrown baby carriages.

It was a terrible disappointment when salt no longer came in cloth sacks, but had to be purchased in boxes and heavy pulp bags. My daughter never had a salt baby. By the time she had come along, they had vanished from the shelves. Poor kid, she only had dolls, for who can kiss and hug a round cardboard carton, even if it does have a pouring lip?

I can close my eyes and remember how dear those salt babies were, nestling against a friendly child. If I ever get a free pass on that time-travel machine they're always threatening to invent, I'll return to some old crossroads store and bring back a load of salt babies—one for every child I know. ❖

Remembering Orange Crates

By Ardyce H. Samp

My 8-year-old grandson, visiting for the day, declared, "There's nothing to do!" The usual Saturday-afternoon TV schedule of sports and rock music did not interest him, the weather outside was a fright, and the toys we kept on hand for the grandkids were geared for toddlers except for a few outdoor toys.

"What did you play with when you were my age?" Tony inquired.

My mind raced back to my childhood days on the farm, back to the "Dirty '30s," as they were called. There were three girls in our family, and I was oldest. We used our imaginations and anything at hand to fill our playtime. We never ran out of things to do.

"Well, some Saturdays we played house with the orange crates."

"What's orange crates?" asked our wide-eyed visitor. This sparked interest as nothing else had that day. So I told him about orange crates:

Years ago the grocery stores bought oranges to sell and the fruit came packed in big wooden boxes which were called crates. They had heavy wooden bottoms and slats (I gestured with my hands), thin sides of wood with spaces between. Best of all, there was a strong wooden divider in the middle to separate the fruit. People ate lots of oranges in those days because there wasn't much choice of fruit shipped north in wintertime. When the fruit was sold, the grocer gave the boxes to people who asked for them. There were many uses for these wooden crates.

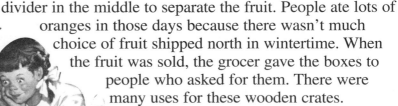

We girls had five or six orange crates in the attic. Attics were big rooms at the top of the house used to store things when they were not needed. On days we had to play indoors, we carried the crates into the living room and played with them.

Sometimes we lined them in a row and pretended we had a train. People rode trains from town to town in those days and lots of store products came on the many trains which ran through our area. We put dolls, teddy bears and little kids in the crates and pushed them around, making tooting and whistling sounds like a train. Mother said we scratched the linoleum and wore out the rug, but she let us play train anyway.

We took turns being conductor and saying "All aboard!" and punching the paper train tickets, which we made out of our tablet paper. This took time, as we made the tickets and pretended to sell them to the passengers.

Some days we played house all day long. We set up the crates on end and made cupboards and tables with them. The divider in the middle made a good shelf for dishes and pretend foods.

Mother had given us a piece of printed material left from dressmaking. We gathered it on a string and tacked it onto the crate to make a curtain for our cupboard. At that time people sometimes made curtains for open shelves to make it look prettier. We made paper doilies for the shelves and used a dish towel to cover the table crate. Many dolls and stuffed animals shared feasts with us. The tea party food was usually soda crackers or graham crackers, marshmallows and little cups of water, but we thought it tasted wonderful.

One of the crates was our pretend stove, as we used our Crayolas to draw stove burners on the top. We pretended to cook our food on this crate stove. We used fruit-jar covers, old pie pans and anything our mother had in the kitchen for the kettles and plates. Our real china dishes were in the china cupboard and were too good to use for playing orange crate house.

Sometimes we played grocery store, I explained. This was a biggie. We begged cans and boxes from Mother's kitchen. We made store shelves with the crates and put the food or stock on the shelves. One crate was laid flat and served as the store counter.

Tony listened, utterly fascinated. He thought awhile and then lamented, "You sure were lucky to have crates to play with!"

We wrote on a grocery sales pad, which we made, and wrote down the order or the lists of items the customer wanted to buy. We took turns playing clerk and customer. For money we used big buttons and we also made dollars out of paper. This took time to make, so we had plenty of things to do. We even had a toy telephone, so we wrote down orders for groceries pretend people wanted to buy and we would take turns delivering these things.

Peach-canning season in the summertime was also fun, as our mother canned many crates of peaches for our winter desserts. Peach crates were smaller, and flat. The sides were about 6 inches high. They were made of wood, but were not as strong as orange crates, but we could sit on them and stretch our legs out.

Since these crates were in plentiful supply, we could take them apart and use the wood to build marvelous things. We salvaged nails and borrowed the kitchen hammer—it wasn't big enough to hurt us—and we pounded away the hours building our secret projects.

My sister always built an airplane out of peach crates. She made a propeller out of thin wood and nailed it to the front of the crate. She sat in her homemade plane for hours and traveled around the world in her imagination.

Peaches were canned in August, so kids could play with the crates outside and Mother was happy as it kept her kitchen clear of children while she worked with the hot jars of fruit. The ends of the peach crates were used as markers for home plate and bases for our three-member ball team. Uses for these crates never ended. When we were finished playing with them, they were broken up, as the wood made good kindling in the wood cooking stove.

∽

Tony listened, utterly fascinated. He picked up his new Transformer toy and began making it into a space-age creature. He thought awhile and then lamented, "You sure were lucky to have crates to play with!" ❖

Homemade Toys & Other Curiosities

By Glenn Conley

My younger sister and I were raised during the "hard times" of the early 1930s. In those years it was difficult to keep the mortgage paid up and food on the table, and we children knew it.

I cannot forget my parents' shame at being "on relief." They wouldn't carry groceries into the house until after dark, and they carefully removed all the NRA labels from our clothing. We children were cautioned never to mention that our family was "getting something for nothing."

My sister and I had few possessions or toys with which to entertain ourselves—except books. We were allowed as many as we could read, but most of them we read two or three times each. During long summers, however, we needed other things to occupy our time, so our parents simply taught us to make our own toys.

My father's knowledge of what it took to entertain a boy was endless. He had grown up on a farm and had helped in his father's blacksmith shop. He could spot the best forked limb among the maple trees around our house, and quickly cut it to size and notch grooves in the top ends. Meanwhile, I would hunt through the garage for an old inner tube and the ball of "staging twine," as he called it. With two strips of rubber, some string and a soft piece of leather from an old shoe, those stubby, sun-browned hands could fashion a beautiful slingshot in short order.

> *With two strips of rubber, some string and a soft piece of leather from an old shoe, those hands could fashion a slingshot in short order.*

It was always given to me with a warning to "Be careful and keep out of meanness with it." That meant, "Don't let the rock hit your finger when shooting, and don't break any windows or fire at the neighbor's cat."

There were also homemade bows and arrows, and a device called a sling with which even a small boy could throw a fist-size rock with terrific force but no real accuracy. I'll never understand how David slew Goliath with one of those contraptions.

My mother lived in constant fear when I had one of these weapons.

It usually ended up with her demanding that I turn it over because of some damage I'd inflicted. I'll bet that before I grew up she had a dresser drawer full of those things. She would not destroy them, I would not ask for them, and Father kept building new ones.

And yet she also contributed. During the winter months mostly, when we were underfoot and complained of having nothing to do, she taught us to pass a string through two holes of a large button, tie it together, loop the string around both hands, and then pull and let loose. The button would whirl back and forth and emit a curious whirring noise.

There were homemade darts, too, and these caused much concern on her part. Each required a kitchen match, a small needle and a bit of newspaper. We lit the match, then quickly blew it out. Into the blackened end, we pressed the eye of the needle. Then, with a razor blade or sharp knife, we slit the other end of the match just once and inserted two pieces of paper measuring about 1 x ½ inch. We bent these at right angles to each other to give the "dart" a stabilizing tail. The darts sailed beautifully, and stuck in furniture and walls almost as easily as they did in the paper targets Mom provided— thus her concern.

Remember the round wafer of wax or paraffin that was poured in the top of a jar of homemade jelly? My mother saved these and used them to make another toy. She drilled a hole in the center and then trimmed and flattened the wax to fit the end of a large spool. Then she passed a rubber band through the wax and the spool and secured it with a whole kitchen match on the wax end, and half a match at the other end. When we turned the whole match to wind up the rubber band and then released the spool on the floor, it would crawl along. This rig was tricky to build and balky to run, but it helped pass many hours.

Then there was the trick with the baking soda can. In those days, baking soda came in a red can about the size of a soda pop can, but with a removable lid. We drilled two small holes half an inch apart in the center of each end and passed a rubber band through them.

A bolt about half as long as the can was

wide was tied to one strand of the rubber band inside and in the center. When the can was rolled across the floor, the suspended bolt would wind tension on the rubber band. With a little practice, we could roll the can halfway across the dining room floor and it would return to us under its own power.

We could make dozens of things from paper, and of course we made our own kites and flew them in the spring. By folding paper we created marvelous little items—airplanes, curious boxes of different sizes, hats, trees, and a gadget that, when moved through the air in a throwing motion, would pop loudly.

And who doesn't remember wrapping tissue paper around a comb, pressing it to the lips and humming a tune?

I believe an entire book could be written about our homemade toys and curiosities. We have passed some of these things along to our children, but in this day of toy technology I'm afraid most of the charm of making things for yourself is not appreciated—another "sign of the times." ❖

Homemade toys many times included rocking horses. Mike and Mabel Huffman of Centerville, Iowa, made this one with just a hack saw for their son Dennis in 1946. They added a leather saddle, blanket and harness, and the rocking horse was good for several children before it was retired.

Gardens of the Great Depression

By Alyce Potts

Remember the "Depression plants" our mothers tended with loving care in the '30s? For us Minnesota natives, these plants were all the rage as most housewives were unable to keep ferns or other houseplants warm enough when it was below zero outside.

It was always fascinating to watch the "plants" grow on a few pieces of coal. When drops of food coloring were added, they were much prettier than real houseplants.

When my children were in elementary school in the early '50s, each teacher set aside some time for "sharing time." My young daughter wore me thin looking for something new to bring to school. Sharing time was her favorite subject.

While going through my drawers one day I happened to find a copy of the recipe for Depression plants from Mrs. Stewart's Bluing. Bluing was used for washing clothes and as a substitute for ink. Many older ladies used it to take the yellow out of their white hair. It also made beautiful Depression plants.

It was fascinating to watch the "plants" grow. When drops of food coloring were added, they were much prettier than real houseplants.

By then I was living in California and could find no coal like we'd burned in our furnace in Minnesota. So I experimented with lumps of charcoal and found that the recipe worked just fine.

Her class was thrilled with my daughter's "new invention" when she shared it at school. Her classmates' mothers phoned me constantly to find out the secret ingredients. Finally I got the bright idea of selling the recipe by mail.

The local post office was 2 miles from my home. I began my business by renting a post office box for $4 per month. Then I was confronted with legal requirements, so I had a notice put in the paper: "DBA (doing business as) Charcoal Gardens." I had a limited budget, but I finally found a new printing company that was willing to print 1,000 copies of the recipe with envelopes to match for $35.

Next I needed to find customers willing to pay 25 cents per copy. Four months and $12 later, my tiny ad for "Charcoal Gardens" was under the "Hobbies" listing in a national magazine. The magazine barely hit the newsstands before I began making daily trips to the post office for recipe requests.

I had visions of finding my mailbox full, but in the next six months I received only 36 letters—and 36 quarters. The postal rate was 6 cents at the time, and I ended up with a total income of $6.84.

Eventually I decided my project was a lost cause, and I went out of business. About a year later I received a lovely letter from a lady in Australia asking for the recipe; her request included an Australian quarter. My postage to return the recipe to her was 50 cents.

By this time I was dreading one more joke about my "flourishing mail-order business." I would burst into tears just at the mention of "sharing time." My only consolation was that I'd been able to deduct my losses from our income tax.

A few years ago, when two of my nieces began teaching elementary school, I presented them each with 50 copies of the recipe as a Christmas joke. Whenever I look in one of those storage boxes in the garage and see the other 850 copies—with envelopes to match—they remind me of my first and last business adventure, and the Good Old Days.

Directions for Charcoal Gardens

In a glass dish place *several lumps of charcoal or soft coal.* (Do not use charcoal briquettes.) Over this pour *2 tablespoons water, 2 tablespoons table salt and 2 tablespoons liquid household bluing.*

The next morning, add *2 additional tablespoons salt* to the top of the charcoal.

In 24 hours a beautiful flowerlike growth will appear. To make it even more beautiful, add *drops of food coloring* to each lump.

On the third day, pour into the bottom of the dish *2 tablespoons salt, 2 tablespoons water and 2 tablespoons bluing.* Watch the flowers bloom mysteriously on the charcoal. Add drops of food color at any time for unusual effects.

To keep your Charcoal Garden growing, add additional water, salt and bluing from time to time. ❖

Some ways of having fun have changed little over the years. It's just as thrifty to enjoy making a snowman today as it was at the turn of the century (above). But when was the last time you saw a rousing hoop race (below)? And while little girls might still play jacks (bottom), it's certainly not as common as it once was.

Shooter

By Rudy Mancini

My first name is Rudy, but my friends called me Shooter. It was a well-deserved nickname. My aim was deadly, my desire to win ruthless and uncompromising. I broke hearts and shattered dreams. I did what no other kid in town had done—I won the Washington Township Marble Competition twice in a row. That's how I got the name Shooter.

The annual marble competition, sponsored by our local newspaper, was open to any public-school student up through the eighth grade. It was a stellar event that every marble-playing kid dreamed of winning. The first time I won, it was a pair of brown leather hightop boots (including a sheath with Barlow knife). The second time my prize was a pump-action Daisy air rifle. A runner-up received a sack of 50 marbles.

Then the word came out that the upcoming tournament would offer a new Stanley bicycle as first prize. This made every kid in town a contestant. Except for Fat Freddie, whose parents owned the local grocery store, no kid in my neighborhood even owned a bicycle.

Any kid who grew up during the '30s was easily hooked on a variety of those fascinating games of colored glass.

Any kid who grew up during the '30s was easily hooked on a variety of those fascinating games of colored glass. It had become a popular Depression-era diversion that made one forget the meatless meals and the drudgery of being poor. Even the most indigent kid could eventually scrape up a dime, the purchase price of a small onion sack of marbles. Then by "playing for keeps," a youngster could build (or soon forfeit) a small fortune in glassies, spirals and onionskins.

There was a sudden magic in that circle scratched with a Barlow knife in the wet spring earth. The thrill of winning your opponents' marbles was enhanced by the possible threat of loss. It was like the rush you might get when wagering your last coin in a high-stakes poker game. And as your collection of marbles increased, so did your social status. A winner, with his bag bulging with agates, could strut away from the game, his knees muddied, his knuckles scratched and sore, and be proud to be dubbed the Shooter.

It's like 1938 or '39. I'm in the eighth grade of Wiley Avenue Grade School, and it's my last opportunity to play in the upcoming marble

competition and win that Stanley bicycle. I rested on my laurels, confident that I was unbeatable. What I didn't know was that one of my opponents, instead of lounging around a potbellied stove all winter, listening to the radio, was down in a cold, damp root cellar practicing shots with a younger brother.

Well, that special day in July finally arrived and things went along pretty much as I expected. Only I and a most unlikely opponent were left to fight it out like two gunfighters facing off at the OK Corral.

The final game was called bull-in-the-ring. Both players put up five marbles each. The judges added one, and the 11 agates were centered in a 12-foot circle. My rival fired first. The onionskin lifted with perfecting trajectory, landing—splat!—dead center, scattering marbles every which way. My heart picked up a beat when three went outside the circle, and my opponent took two more before missing.

I, too, ran a string of five. I was sitting in the catbird's seat, I thought. One more marble would take the bike, and it still was my turn at a fairly easy shot, the agate lying maybe a foot or so from the line.

My heart was pounding. My knees were jelly as I kneeled, aimed and fired … my spiral shooter striking the marble off-center skittering the marble sideways across the ring. I didn't realize it was a miss, staying just a few inches inside the circle, until I head a collective gasp, followed by a chorus of "Oh, noooo, Shooooter, I don't believe it!"

I could already see my opponent riding that bike; anyone could make that shot with their eyes closed. I couldn't watch, but when I heard that sharp crack of glass against glass, I knew the game was over. My dream of a bicycle was still just a dream.

The other losers and I stood around with long faces as one of the judges appeared with the winner's prize, a brand-new, fire-engine–red Stanley bicycle with whitewall balloon tires. What a beauty, I thought as I watched him turn the handlebars over to its new owner.

"Can this bike be exchanged?" said the new champion.

"What do you mean?" said the judge.

"Well, this is a boy's bike. In case you have not noticed, I'm a girl," she said proudly, flipping a ponytail over her shoulder.

"I'm sorry, Sue Ann, but it can't be exchanged," said the judge. "But, look, you can take it to any bike shop and they can convert it to your liking. Actually," he continued, "you could take a hacksaw—"

Mr. Greene was still blabbing away when Sue Ann pushed through the crowd with her prize, ran alongside it for a few seconds, then swung aboard the seat and pedaled away.

You know, Sue Ann never changed a thing on that bike. She rode it around town for years, kind of flaunting it, reminding us guys that a gutsy, 90-pound girl in pigtails took "all the marbles" and beat out a kid they used to call Shooter. ❖

I'm pictured with some of my fellow marble players in 1938. I'm the third from the left.

Depression-Era Sock Doll

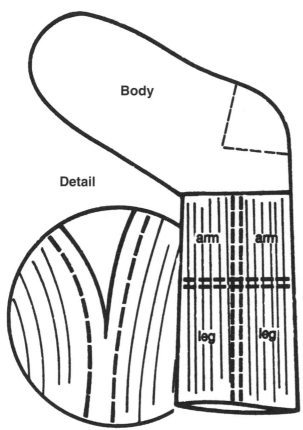

Body

Detail

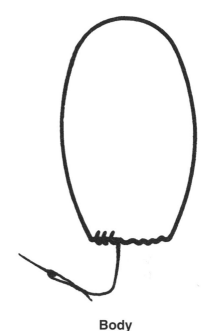

Body

Stuff firmly and turn under opening and stitch shut.

Machine-stitch or hand-sew on the dotted lines; then cut between the stitching.

Arm and Leg

Turn each of the four cuff pieces inside out. Stuff each and sew opening shut. Wrap a double thread around where the wrist or ankle should go. Knot off.

Wrap a double thread around the body several times where the neck should go. Sew on arms and legs securely. Add buttons for eyes, or embroider features as desired. Hair can be made from yarn.

The Circus Is Coming!

By Doreen LaChambre Houston

Winter of 1933, as mean and harsh as the Depression, seemed to last forever. The work Daddy did get that year came mostly from W.P.A. jobs, and he spent a lot of days digging into Missoula's frozen streets with a pick and shovel to repair frozen water lines. Winter eventually gave way to spring, and Daddy managed to get our bill at the corner grocery store current as summer burst into our lives.

I heard the news first. The circus was coming to town! There was little money to spend on anything so trivial. However, I felt happy and excited. I knew Daddy would take us all to see the animals.

The night the fancy painted boxcars pulled within sight of Missoula, our family delighted in a special preview of the circus. We hurried across Higgins Avenue Bridge, through town, and past my Aunt Bernie's house in the Orchard Homes, to where the circus train had settled on a railroad siding.

Just as we arrived, some dusty men slid open a boxcar door and began unloading animals into the field sucked dry by the relentless hot wind. The elephants came out first. "They will help unload the equipment," Daddy told us, as if he knew special secrets about circuses. The huge, gray animals lumbered down the ramp. The gentle look in their eyes surprised me, and I wanted to run up and hug one.

The elephants came out first. "They will help unload the equipment," Daddy told us, as if he knew special secrets about circuses.

We wandered farther down the tracks and saw the roustabouts. They yanked out trunks from the cars, along with armloads of bright costumes and other trappings. We didn't stand there too long. Clothes without people in them didn't interest us.

A sunburned, frazzle-haired blonde fussed over a group of little yapping dogs. They jumped around the woman's spindly legs. I stared at her feet. She wore the highest high-heeled shoes I had ever seen. "The dogs do cute little tricks," Mama told us.

I suppose if they had been dressed in ruffled collars they might have been cute, but undressed I just saw barking mutts. They couldn't begin

The elephants helped load and unload train flat cars and boxcars, as shown by this cover from the July 1946 issue of Railroad Magazine.

to compare with my own Bingo at home.

We turned around just in time to watch a man shimmy up a ladder. He threw open another boxcar full of creatures which made growling, snarling noises. The sounds made the hair on my scalp go stiff and tingly. The men yelled at the cats, but they cautiously lifted the wire crates from the train and onto wheeled wooden platforms. Two lions rocked back and forth, blinking into the sun. Again, the men reached into the blackness of the boxcar, inched out another crate, and jerked it to the ground. It

was the prison of a snarling tiger who looked beautiful wearing his colored stripes.

The boxcars with pictures of bears painted on their sides stood empty. I felt disappointed, but as we walked through the field, we saw large cages next to a tent. The cages, dimmed in the shade of the hastily erected canvas structures, held the bears. We couldn't really see them very well, but we could hear the "woofs" and experienced their primitive smell.

The sounds of pounding reached us. Daddy grinned when we came near two black men beating stakes for the Big Top. The red color of the fading sun glistened on their backs as they pounded away. Bam, BAM! Bam, BAM! Bam, BAM! Striking the stake in perfect rhythm and cadence, the men chanted as they worked. We watched for a long time because this was Daddy's favorite circus thing.

All too soon it was time to start the long walk back home. Without knowing it, we found ourselves walking directly behind a parade of elephants. They were heading for the irrigation ditch by Aunt Bernie's house … to my special ditch! We stood nearby as the elephants sucked the cool water into their trunks, then sprayed each other. Having elephants at my ditch makes it even more special than if that ditch were banked in layers of gold, I thought. After a few minutes, the handlers prodded the elephants with long sticks to turn them back to the tents. My parents turned my two big sisters and me toward home.

The next day proved to be a scorcher, but Daddy promised we would return to the circus to walk around again. I think he wanted to soak up the sights and sounds and smells of the circus as much as we girls did. Hundreds of people were already lined up to enter the Big Top when we arrived.

A carnival had set up after we left the night before. Now the air was filled with tantalizing smells of hamburgers, popcorn, hot dogs. We knew Daddy couldn't afford any of those things and we didn't ask. Much to our surprise, Mama said, "You can each go on two rides."

The flashing lights on the merry-go-round and Ferris wheel were so brilliant that they made my eyes water, and I generously gave my sisters, Joan and Elaine, my two turns, because even looking at the painted horses whirling by made my stomach churn.

I skipped away. Mama called out for me to wait, but I didn't. She caught me by my shirt and jerked me back to stay with the rest of the family. I only got a glimpse of the fat lady. A man in tight, orange pants jumped onto another stage and swallowed a stick of fire. Farther on down the line, hideous screams erupted from the Tent of Horrors.

People began pushing into the Big Top.

Daddy didn't have tickets for the circus and he drew us away from the tent flaps. He led us back to the carnival area where he bought us all a hot dog. No food ever tasted better than that unexpected treat! I ate slowly, savoring the mustard-smeared wiener and stale bun. I hoped mine would last longer than my sisters'.

I spotted the gentle giants again standing behind one of the tents, bound with heavy chains linked from their ankles to a big stake driven into the ground. Their huge heads swayed to and fro in impatient boredom.

As we walked back near the Big Top we heard music and clapping. Daddy whispered something to Mama, then ducked under the edge of the tent. We three girls froze in rigid surprise and looked up at Mama. In a flash, Daddy's grinning face emerged. "I can sneak us all in," he said, but Mama shook her head, no, no, no!

We left the magical arena once again. I skipped along, recrossing the long bridge leading toward home. The air had turned sweet and cool. Oh, it had been a wonderful day! No little girl could ever, ever have had a better time at the circus! ❖

The Talking Hollow Tree

By Robert Gay

When I was a young boy of 6 and older, living on a farm in rural New England, it was my duty each late afternoon during the summer to go after the cows in a very large pasture and drive them back to the barn for milking. Most often I would find them grazing in a section we called "the old swamp."

The swamp was a clearing in the woods that had bountiful green grass, a small freshwater stream and a giant hollow tree that towered above all other trees in the area. My dad had told me that the tree measured 5 feet at its base, and was completely hollow to a height of 40 feet or more.

When I grew up I found that his measurements were right. The tree also had a round hole in its side, about 5 feet up from the base, that was just a little larger than my head. I could look into that dark, mysterious hole and see the hollow trunk. I learned at an early age that if I shouted into the hole my voice would echo back, and I pretended the tree was talking to me. I would yell in the hole, "Hello there" and I would hear "Hello there, hello there, hello there" from the echo.

During those years it became a ritual: When I went to the swamp to gather the cows and drive them home, I would pick up a large stick and pound on the tree to scare out any animals that might be living in it. Then I would get up the courage to peek into the hole and ask the tree all kinds of boyish questions, such as had it seen any Indians? I'd shout the word "Indians" and I would hear "Indians? Indians? Indians?" as though it were trying to recall. Sometimes I would shout naughty words into the hole and giggle as they echoed back to me.

When I was 12, my mother died. Two years later my father sold the farm and all its timberland to the state. They eventually set out young pine trees on all of the open land, turning the land into a state forest. The last time I ever went after the cows, I spent more time than usual with the hollow tree and left with a sadness in my heart. I was leaving my make-believe friend in the swamp, but I did promise to come back and visit someday.

When I was in my late 20s, with a family and home of my own, I would use hunting as an excuse to go back to the land of my youth.

Each time I went back, I found the land fast growing up into wilderness, with all landmarks disappearing. Yet, as I hunted rather aimlessly, I'd often find myself near or in the old swamp, where I would find the hollow tree and once again talk into the hole.

The tree did not seem to have changed much except that the hole was a little larger and was rotting around its edges. It still echoed my voice.

Eventually my work took me to another state. When I was in my late 40s, I decided to go hunting just one more time on the land I had roamed as a young boy. When I arrived, there was nothing but pine forests and wilderness everywhere I looked, and no landmarks at all. After an hour or so I came across a stream that I was sure came from the old swamp. I followed it and hunted upstream until I was in the swamp, but I could not see the hollow tree.

My eyes fell on a strange mound about three feet tall and perhaps 40 feet long. I dug the toe of my boot into the mound and realized it was the hollow tree. It had fallen and was burying itself in its own rotting wood, decayed leaves and moss. I bent down and touched it and left with some tears in my eyes, knowing my old friend was deteriorating into the earth forever. I'm sure if there is a place in heaven for special trees, my friend is up there, waiting for me to visit one final time. ❖